Headway

Academic Skills

Listening, Speaking, and Study Skills

LEVEL 3 **Student's Book**

Richard Harrison
Series Editors: Liz and John Soars

OXFORD

CONTENTS

1 Learning and intelligence

LISTENING How to be a successful student   p4
Listening for gist   Listening for specific information
Intelligence and learning   p5
Critical thinking (1) Defining terms   Understanding the language of graphs

SPEAKING Assessing study habits   p8
Assessing yourself
Taking part in a discussion   p9
Taking turns in a discussion

2 Health and fitness

LISTENING Healthy alternatives   p12
Critical thinking (2) Evaluating evidence   Key vocabulary for listening
Identifying speakers' opinions
Healthy body, healthy mind   p14
Note-taking (1) Techniques
RESEARCH References   p15

SPEAKING Organizing a presentation   p16
Presentations (1) Structure
Introducing a presentation   p17
Presentations (2) Introductions

3 Changing cities

LISTENING The history of a city   p20
Activating what you know   Critical thinking (3) Fact or opinion?
Eco-cities   p22
Note-taking (2) Linear notes   Recognizing signposts

SPEAKING Expressing opinions   p24
Expressing opinions
Organizing content   p25
Presentations (3) Organizing the main content

4 Issues in agriculture

LISTENING Feed the world   p28
Recognizing causes and solutions   References to earlier comments
Malawi – a success story   p30
Listening to an illustrated talk

SPEAKING Discussing pros and cons   p32
Critical thinking (4) Seeing a problem from all sides
Presenting facts and figures   p33
Presentations (4) Facts and figures

5 Global culture

LISTENING Are we all becoming the same?   p36
Listening for questions   Critical thinking (5) Anecdotal evidence
Coffee and culture   p38
Recognizing what information is important

SPEAKING Conducting an interview   p40
Conducting interviews
Presenting results   p41
Presenting with graphics

6 History and heritage

LISTENING What is World Heritage?   p44
Establishing criteria
Conserving a historical site   p46
Critical thinking (6) Detecting points of view

SPEAKING Presenting data   p48
Summarizing data from a table
Concluding your presentation   p49
Presentations (5) The conclusion
RESEARCH Using the Internet   p47

7 Developments in architecture

LISTENING Airports around the world   p52
Making inferences
Green skyscrapers   p54
Recognizing the plan of a talk   Mind mapping

SPEAKING Supporting your argument   p56
Critical thinking (7) Supporting a point of view
Describing visuals   p57
Preparing visuals

8 The sports industry

LISTENING Sports sponsorship   p60
Recognizing the structure of an interview
The science of sport   p61
Reviewing and organizing notes
RESEARCH Keywords   p63

SPEAKING Interviewing   p64
Successful interviews
Logical organization   p65
Presentations (6) Logical organization   Establishing rapport

9 Global statistics

LISTENING Trends in world population   p68
Interpreting data in maps   Recognizing tentative language
Is life getting better?   p70
Recognizing lecture styles   Getting the most out of visuals

SPEAKING Presenting results   p72
Describing results in a presentation   Analyzing data critically
Discussing a survey report   p73
Presentating a survey report

10 Technological advances

LISTENING The end of books?   p78
Critical listening
Technology of the future   p70
Dealing with fast speech   Active listening: asking questions

SPEAKING Giving and supporting opinions   p80
Recognizing an opposing view
Giving a presentation in new technology   p81
Presentations (7) Delivery

VOCABULARY DEVELOPMENT Using a dictionary   p10   **REVIEW**   p11
Knowing a word

VOCABULARY DEVELOPMENT Recording vocabulary   p18   **REVIEW**   p19
Recording vocabulary
Using pictures and diagrams

VOCABULARY DEVELOPMENT Learning academic vocabulary   p26   **REVIEW**   p27
Academic words

VOCABULARY DEVELOPMENT Collocations   p34   **REVIEW**   p35
Collocations

VOCABULARY DEVELOPMENT Word formation (1)   p42   **REVIEW**   p43
Suffixes

VOCABULARY DEVELOPMENT Word formation (2)   p50   **REVIEW**   p51
Prefixes

VOCABULARY DEVELOPMENT Subject-specific vocabulary   p58   **REVIEW**   p59
Learning subject-specific vocabulary

VOCABULARY DEVELOPMENT Word families   p66   **REVIEW**   p67
Word families

VOCABULARY DEVELOPMENT Multiple meanings   p74   **REVIEW**   p75
Formal and informal register

VOCABULARY DEVELOPMENT Register   p82   **REVIEW**   p83
Formal and Informal

1 Learning and intelligence

LISTENING SKILLS Listening for gist • Listening for specific information • Critical thinking (1) Defining terms
• Understanding the language of graphs
SPEAKING SKILLS Assessing yourself • Taking turns in a discussion
VOCABULARY DEVELOPMENT Knowing a word

LISTENING How to be a successful student

1 Look at the students in the photo. They have just graduated. Work in groups and discuss the questions below. Then share your group's ideas with the rest of the class.

1 What are the study habits of successful students?
2 What are the habits of unsuccessful students?

Add your ideas to the table.

successful students:	unsuccessful students:
plan their time	are late with assignments

2 **Read STUDY SKILL** ⊚ 1.1 Listen to the first part of a talk to new students. What is the gist of what the speaker is saying? Which two of the following general points are covered in the talk?

1 The importance of choosing the right programme of study.
2 What it means to be a successful student.
3 How to prepare yourself for examinations.
4 The differences between university life and school.
5 The role of motivation in studying.

3 ⊚ 1.1 Compare your answers with your partner. Then listen again and check your answers.

> **STUDY SKILL** Listening for gist
>
> Sometimes a listener may just want to get a general idea of what the speaker is saying, not detailed information. Listening for the general idea is also called listening for gist.

4 **Read STUDY SKILL** 🔊 1.2 Listen to the second part of the talk. The speaker explains what students should do in order to be better students. List the main points in column A of the table below. Check your answers with a partner.

A advice	B language signals
time management	One of the most important skills is ...

STUDY SKILL Listening for specific information

Sometimes we listen for specific information, for example:
- times, dates, facts and figures.
- main points in a list.
- an argument / a line of reasoning.

Important information is often signalled by the choice of words, for example:
- *One of the most important skills is ...*
- *Another piece of advice is ...*
- *I'd like to point out that ...*
- *It's important to remember that ...*

Speakers sometimes speak more slowly and clearly to show that some points are important.

5 🔊 1.2 Listen again to the second part of the talk. What phrases did the speaker use to signal the main points? Write them in column B of the table above.

Intelligence and learning

1 One way of measuring intelligence (or 'IQ') is by tests. Try the quiz below to test your intelligence.

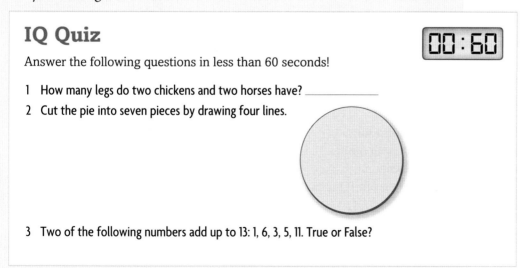

IQ Quiz

00:60

Answer the following questions in less than 60 seconds!

1 How many legs do two chickens and two horses have? _____
2 Cut the pie into seven pieces by drawing four lines.

3 Two of the following numbers add up to 13: 1, 6, 3, 5, 11. True or False?

2 Discuss your results with a partner. What do tests like these try to measure? Are they successful?

3 Read STUDY SKILL Work in groups. Discuss the questions.

1 What is intelligence? Can you give a definition?
2 Is intelligence inherited from parents or is it learned?
3 Is intelligence related to brain size?
4 Do you know people who are intelligent but who haven't been very well educated? In what ways are they intelligent?
5 Is there more than one kind of intelligence?

4 Look at the definitions below. Tick (✓) the option which is closest to your understanding of the word. Improve the definition you choose if you can.

1 *Intelligence* is the ability to …
  ☐ deal with practical everyday problems.
  ☐ pass examinations with high scores.
  ☐ think quickly and find solutions.
2 *Success* means …
  ☐ being respected in society.
  ☐ having a job with a high salary.
  ☐ having good qualifications.
3 An *educated* person is one who …
  ☐ has read many books on a variety of subjects.
  ☐ has been to university and obtained qualifications.
  ☐ treats other people fairly.
4 A *healthy* person is one who …
  ☐ never sees a doctor or goes to hospital.
  ☐ has a positive outlook on life.
  ☐ exercises a lot and has a good diet.

5 Write definitions for these words.

1 poverty   2 biased   3 logical

6 Read the text below about IQ tests. Check any vocabulary that is new to you. Then decide if statements 1–4 are True (T) or False (F).

> ## Measuring intelligence
>
> Originally, IQ, or Intelligence Quotient, was used to detect children of lower intelligence in order to place them in special education programmes. The first IQ tests were designed to compare a child's intelligence to what his or her intelligence 'should be' as relative to the child's age. Today, IQ testing is used mainly for adults. The tests attempt to measure an adult's true mental potential, unbiased by culture. The tests compare the scores of one adult to the scores of other adults who have taken the same test. The average score (IQ) is set at 100, so a person who scores more than 100 is 'more intelligent' than average and someone who scores below 100 is said to be less intelligent. However, some people think that IQ tests only measure a narrow range of intelligence, for example mathematical and logical intelligence. They may also be biased by cultural factors.

1 The original IQ test was used mainly for testing adults. _____
2 Today's tests compare the scores of one adult with others. _____
3 A score of 100 means a person is very intelligent. _____
4 Some people think that there may be cultural bias in IQ tests. _____

STUDY SKILL Critical thinking (1) Defining terms

One part of critical thinking is being clear about the exact meaning of the words we use.
We need to define the terms we use clearly, so for example, if we are discussing intelligence, we must first decide:

■ What is *intelligence*?
■ What do we mean by an *intelligent* person?

Different people have different ideas of what words such as *intelligence* or *intelligent* mean.

7 **Read STUDY SKILL** 1.3 Listen to the first part of the lecture on multiple intelligences. Which of the following graphs does the lecturer describe?

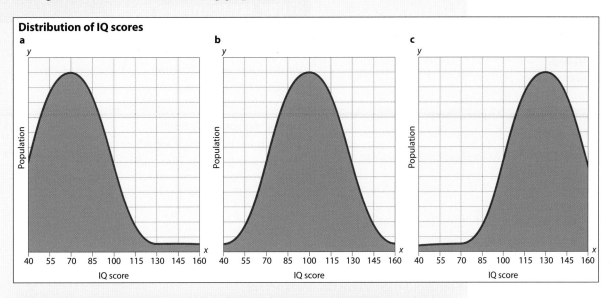

Distribution of IQ scores

STUDY SKILL Understanding the language of graphs

Make sure you are familiar with the basic language of graphs. Some of the key terms are:

vertical axis, horizontal axis, curve, distribution, peak, range

It is especially important to understand:

- what the graph is meant to show, e.g. the title and dates.
- what the vertical axis measures.
- what the horizontal axis measures.

8 1.4 Listen to the second part of the lecture on multiple intelligences. As you listen, match the types of intelligence (1–7) with the features (a–g).

A types of intelligence:	B features
1 ☐ Linguistic	a read maps and plans effectively
2 ☐ Logical-mathematical	b move the body well: sports, dancing, making things
3 ☐ Spatial	c use words well in speaking, writing, etc.
4 ☐ Bodily-kinaesthetic	d understand other people and their problems
5 ☐ Musical	e understand himself/herself and reflect
6 ☐ Interpersonal	f sing, compose or play instruments
7 ☐ Intrapersonal	g deal with numbers, scientific or legal problems

9 1.5 Listen to the last part of the lecture on the implications of this theory. Complete the handout below with information from the lecture.

Implications of Gardner's theory …

1 For education and society:
Schools focus most attention on _____
But schools should also focus on _____
2 For teachers:
Teachers should _____

SPEAKING Assessing study habits

1 [Read STUDY SKILL] Decide what your strengths and weaknesses are. Add to the list below.

- Good at working with others.
- Note-taking in lectures.
- Meeting deadlines.

2 Think about your study habits. Answer these questions and write notes.

1 When do you like to study? **At weekends in the mornings.**
2 Where do you like to study?
3 Do you take regular breaks?
4 Do you take notes while studying?
5 Do you make plans for your study time and free time?
6 Do you like to study alone or in a group?

3 ◎ 1.6 Listen to Sarah and Andrew talking about their study habits. As you listen, complete the table with information about their strengths, weaknesses and study habits.

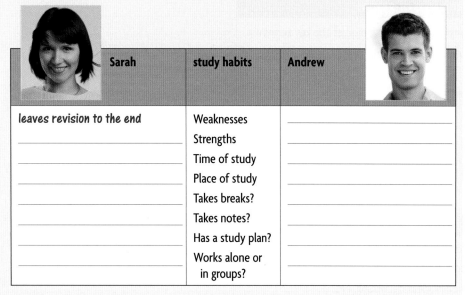

Sarah	study habits	Andrew
leaves revision to the end	Weaknesses	
	Strengths	
	Time of study	
	Place of study	
	Takes breaks?	
	Takes notes?	
	Has a study plan?	
	Works alone or in groups?	

4 Work in pairs or small groups. Discuss your strengths, weaknesses and study habits. Use the expressions in the Language Bank and your notes from exercises 1 and 2.

LANGUAGE BANK Describing yourself

Strengths and weaknesses
I'm good at giving presentations.
I find speaking in seminars quite easy.
One of my strengths / weaknesses is researching on the Internet.
I'm not so good at checking grammar mistakes.
What I find difficult is taking notes.

Habits
I always / usually / never work better at night.
I like / hate / prefer getting up early to study.
What I hate doing is checking spellings.

Taking part in a discussion

1 Rate yourself for each type of intelligence. 1 = 'I am weak' and 5 = 'I am strong' in this type of intelligence.

Linguistic intelligence	1 2 3 4 5
Logical-mathematical intelligence	1 2 3 4 5
Spatial intelligence	1 2 3 4 5
Bodily-kinaesthetic intelligence	1 2 3 4 5
Musical intelligence	1 2 3 4 5
Interpersonal intelligence	1 2 3 4 5
Intrapersonal intelligence	1 2 3 4 5

A discussion group

2 Compare your results with your partner. Explain your choices.

3 **Read STUDY SKILL** 🔊 1.7 Listen to this extract from a discussion on multiple intelligences. How many examples can you find of the following actions? Write the examples in the box.

action	examples
Handing over to other people Interrupting Holding the floor	

STUDY SKILL Taking turns in a discussion

In a discussion, it is important to take your turn, and also let others take their turns. You should practise how to:
- 'take the floor' or interrupt another speaker.
- 'hold the floor' and stop another person interrupting.
- 'hand over' to other speakers.

---

4 Study these discussion questions and make notes.
1 Does the theory of multiple intelligences make sense?
2 Which intelligences do you accept as likely? Give reasons.
3 Which intelligences (if any) are you not sure about? Give reasons.
4 How do you rate yourself, using the seven types of intelligence?
5 What implications are there for students and for teachers?

5 Work in groups of three or four. Discuss the questions from exercise 4 for about ten minutes. Make sure you contribute fully to the discussion, using the expressions from the Language Bank. Try to:
1 interrupt at least once.
2 stop interruptions at least once.
3 hand over to another student.

6 Each group should report on their discussion to the rest of the class.
1 How did you respond to the questions? Summarize the views of the group.
2 How successful was the discussion? Did all members participate?

LANGUAGE BANK
Language for discussions

Taking the floor / Interrupting
Could I just make a point ...?
I'd like to add something here ...
I agree with ... but I'd just like to say ...
Could I say something here ...?
Yes, but ...!

Holding the floor
Could you hold on ...?
Could I just finish ...?
Well, let me explain ...
Sorry, but I'd just like to finish by saying ...

Handing over to other speakers
What does everyone else think?
Does everyone agree?
What do you think?
Would you like to comment?

VOCABULARY DEVELOPMENT Using a dictionary

1 **Read STUDY SKILL** Study the table. It shows what 'knowing' the word *intelligent* means. Complete the table with information from the dictionary entry.

word	intelligent	
the meaning(s)	having the ability to understand learn and think	
part of speech		
pronunciation		
synonyms	clever, bright, brainy	
antonyms	unintelligent	
collocations	verbs: be, look, seem adv.: extremely, highly, fairly	
forms of the word	intelligence, intelligently, intellectual, intellect, intelligible	

2 Use a dictionary to complete the rest of the table for one of the words in the box.

organize	success	logical	critical

3 Use a dictionary to help you complete the rest of the table below. Then practise saying the words with a partner.

word	stress	word	stress
intelligence intellect intelligent	o O o o	intelligently intellectual intelligible	o o O o o

4 Find the parts of speech of these words related to *intelligent*. Write (n), (adj) or (adv).

intelligent **(adj)**   intelligence ___   intelligently ___
intellect ___   intellectual ___   intelligible ___

5 Complete the sentences with one of the words from exercise 4.

1 This subject seems very difficult but the writer explains it in a way that is completely _____ to the average reader.
2 She looked at me coolly and _____ before answering the question.
3 Kim took an _____ test last week and is waiting for the result.
4 Maria is a very _____ child. Although she is only three, she can already do simple calculations.
5 Einstein was man of considerable _____ . We only need to look at his record as a scientist.
6 Gandhi was a great _____ . He thought deeply about life, the world and the spirit.

---

intellect /ˈɪntəlekt/ *noun* **1** [U] the power of the mind to think and to learn: *a woman of considerable intellect* **2** [C] an extremely intelligent person: *He was one of the most brilliant intellects of his time.*

intellectual¹ /ˌɪntəˈlektʃuəl/ *adj.* **1** (only *before* a noun) connected with a person's ability to think in a logical way and to understand things: *The boy's intellectual development was very advanced for his age.* **2** (used about a person) enjoying activities in which you have to think deeply about sth ▶ **intellectually** *adv.*

intellectual² /ˌɪntəˈlektʃuəl/ *noun* [C] a person who enjoys thinking deeply about things

ˌintelˌlectual 'property *noun* [U] (LAW) an idea, a design, etc. that sb has created and that the law prevents other people from copying: *intellectual property rights*

intelligence ⚬0 **AW** /ɪnˈtelɪdʒəns/ *noun* [U] **1** the ability to understand, learn and think: *a person of normal intelligence* ◇ *an intelligence test* **2** important information about an enemy country

intelligent ⚬0 **AW** /ɪnˈtelɪdʒənt/ *adj.* having or showing the ability to understand, learn and think; clever: *All their children are very intelligent.* ◇ *an intelligent question* ▶ **intelligently** *adv.*

intelligible /ɪnˈtelɪdʒəbl/ *adj.* (used especially about speech or writing) possible or easy to understand **OPP** **unintelligible** ▶ **intelligibility** /ɪnˌtelɪdʒəˈbɪləti/ *noun* [U]

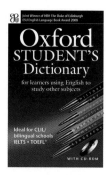

REVIEW

1 🎧 1.8 Listen to a student talking about her academic strengths and weaknesses. Then read the sentences. Are the sentences examples of gist or specific information?

1 She got good marks last year. _____
2 She thinks she is a successful student. _____
3 She has a research paper due on Friday. _____
4 She studies in the library almost every evening. _____
5 She is motivated to do well on the course. _____

2 🎧 1.8 Listen again and correct the sentences.

1 She's just started at university.
2 She's studying Law.
3 She handed in a research paper last week.
4 She doesn't start assignments until the last minute.

3 🎧 1.9 Listen to the presenter and label the graph with the years.

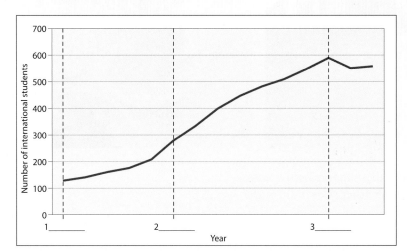

4 Underline the logical response in each mini-dialogue.

1 **Mark:** Does everyone agree?
   Klara: **Could I just finish, please? / Well, not entirely.**

2 **Anna:** … that's why I think there are, in fact, many kinds of intelligence …
   Victor: **I'd like to add something here. / Well, let me explain …**

3 **Carmen:** … Yes Kim, but could I just make a point here?
   Kim: **Could you hold on until I finish, please? / Arthur, what do you think?**

4 **Tom:** Would you like to comment, Greg?
   Greg: **What does everyone else think? / Thank you, Tom. I think …**

5 In small groups, use the prompts to discuss how universities can help students to be successful. Each student should practise interrupting, holding the floor, and handing over to another student.

- Providing resources and support
- Organizing study groups
- Having lecturers available outside of class
- Involving various types of intelligence

2 Health and fitness

LISTENING SKILLS Critical thinking (2) Evaluating evidence • Key vocabulary for listening
• Identifying speakers' opinions • Note-taking (1) Techniques
RESEARCH Referencing
SPEAKING SKILLS Presentations (1) Structure • Presentations (2) Introductions
VOCABULARY DEVELOPMENT Recording vocabulary • Using pictures and diagrams

LISTENING Healthy alternatives?

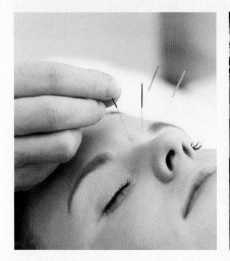

1 🎵 2.1 Look at the photos. What do you know about these therapies? Discuss with a partner. Listen and check your ideas, and put the therapies in the order you hear them.

☐ Hypnosis ☐ Hydrotherapy ☐ Acupuncture ☐ Yoga ☐ Herbal medicine

2 Work in groups. Discuss the questions.

1 Why are alternative therapies popular?
2 Do you believe that alternative therapies work? Why? / Why not?
3 What scientific evidence is there to support your view?

3 **Read STUDY SKILL** Read the claims below. Can you accept them? Work in pairs or small groups, and decide what evidence or what tests are needed to support the claims.

1 Eating fish is good for the brain.
2 The body needs vitamins, so everyone should take vitamin supplements.
3 We need to exercise three times a week for at least 30 minutes.
4 People should not drink coffee as there is a correlation between caffeine intake and heart disease.

STUDY SKILL Critical thinking (2) Evaluating evidence

It is important to evaluate claims. In order to do this you must find and evaluate evidence which can support or refute the claim. Ask questions, for example:

■ What proof is there?
■ Have tests or surveys been carried out?
■ How were the tests carried out?
■ What were the results?

---

4 **Read STUDY SKILL** You are going to listen to a seminar discussion, 'Alternative therapies or evidence-based medicine?' Match the words with the definitions below.

1 ☐ prove (v)   a always behaving in a traditional or normal way
2 ☐ anecdote (n)   b make healthy again after illness
3 ☐ cure (v)   c a short, interesting story about a real event
4 ☐ remission (n)   d when a disease disappears or the condition improves
5 ☐ therapist (n)   e have a connection between two or more things
6 ☐ correlate (v)   f the use of medicine or medical care to help people recover from illness
7 ☐ conventional (adj)   g a person who treats physical or mental illness
8 ☐ treatment (n)   h show that something is true

STUDY SKILL
Key vocabulary for listening

Before you listen to a discussion, a lecture, a presentation, etc. make sure you are familiar with the key vocabulary you may need to understand that topic.

- Search for vocabulary related to the topic (e.g. *alternative medicine – complementary, evidence, treatment*)
- Make sure you recognize the pronunciation (and stress) of the word.

5 **Read STUDY SKILL** (◎) 2.2 Three medical students – Sunil, Lee, and Miriam – have just been to a lecture on 'Alternative therapies or evidence-based medicine'. Listen to the speakers expressing their views on alternative therapies.

1 What are their opinions? Are they in favour, against or undecided?
2 Which speaker has strong views on the subject?
3 Which speakers have more moderate views?

6 (◎) 2.2 Listen to the discussion again. Decide which speaker mentions these points. Write S (Sunil), L (Lee), or M (Miriam).

Which speaker …

1 summarizes Dr Hall's views? ___
2 thinks there is evidence that alternative medicine works? ___
3 claims to have an aunt cured by an alternative therapy? ___
4 doesn't approve of anecdotal evidence? ___
5 says we should keep an open mind on the issue? ___
6 mentions a correlation between herbal medicine and the treatment of diabetes? ___
7 always seems to agree with Dr Hall? ___

anecdotal

scientific

STUDY SKILL Identifying speakers' opinions

When listening to a group discussion, train yourself to:
- identify each of the speakers as they enter into the discussion.
- recognize the speakers by tone of voice or by name throughout the discussion.
- recognize language that signals opinions or beliefs that the speakers may hold, e.g. *In my view … / It seems to me …*
- understand phrases that help identify speakers' attitudes during the discussion, for example:

assertive
That's completely wrong!
It is quite clear that …

neutral
I understand what you are saying, but …
That's true, although …

defensive
Why are you asking me that?
No, I didn't say that.

Healthy body, healthy mind?

1 Read this short text from a university website. It describes a podcast called 'Scientific Research'.

  1 Check any vocabulary that is unfamiliar.

  2 What is the main finding of the research?

  3 What would you like to find out from this podcast? Write six questions.

> ### Physically fit students get better grades
>
> A recent study of school students in the USA shows a correlation between physical fitness and academic performance. It seems that physically fit students do better in Maths, reading and language tests than unfit or overweight students. This week's edition of *Scientific Research* examines these results and asks the question 'What are the implications of this for schools?' The programme also gets the views of some Manchester University students working out in the university gym.

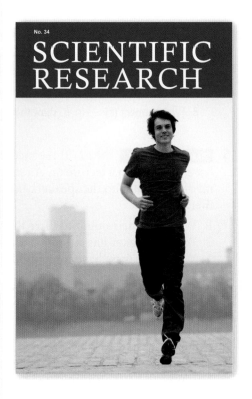

No. 34
SCIENTIFIC RESEARCH

2 🔘 2.3 Listen to the start of the podcast 'Scientific Research'. Give two reasons why students may not be healthy.

3 🔘 2.4 Listen to the rest of the podcast. Decide if these statements are True (T) or False (F).

  1 The tests were carried out at the University of California in the year 2000. ___

  2 The study showed that unfit and overweight students had lower scores in maths, reading and language tests. ___

  3 The results showed a correlation between fitness and diet. ___

  4 Researchers don't know the reasons why exercise helps the brain. ___

  5 Flavia goes to the gym more often than Don. ___

  6 Both of the students who are interviewed find exercise helpful for their studies. ___

4 **Read STUDY SKILL** Read the notes about a different study on the same subject. What is wrong with them? How can you improve them? Discuss with a partner. Then rewrite the notes using the tips in the Study Skill box.

> A study was carried out in Australia by Dwyer and others in 2001. Dwyer comes from Tasmania – which is a small island off the south coast of Australia. From the results, it was seen that there was some correlation between academic performance and fitness. They tested more than 7,500 schoolchildren. The schoolchildren were aged from seven to fifteen years old. They obtained results from questionnaires about physical activity and they also obtained results from fitness tests, for example running and jumping. Academic performance was measured on a five-point scale, from 1 to 5.

> ### STUDY SKILL Note-taking (1) Techniques
>
> When writing notes:
> - don't write in full sentences.
> - use single words or phrases.
> - use abbreviations and symbols: *etc., e.g.,* +, &, ...
> - include only important information and facts and figures.
> - show relationships between information, e.g. using arrows.

5 🔊 2.5 Listen to the podcast again. Complete these notes with facts and figures about the research.

Scientific Research podcast notes

The study:	Researchers: Dr [1]_____ and colleagues, University of [2]_____, [3]_____
Dates of study:	[4]_____ to [5]_____
Number of students:	[6]_____ Male [7]_____ %, Female [8]_____ %
Ethnic groups:	[9]_____
Method:	Weighed students – [10]_____ % overweight
	Students walked/ran 1 mile: Ave. times: boys [11]_____ min; girls [12]_____ min
Results:	Fit students scored [13]_____ than unfit students in tests
	Overweight students scored [14]_____ than 'desirable' weight
Conclusion:	Strong correlation between [15]_____ and academic performance
	Exercise is [16]_____ for [17]_____ performance

---

6 Work in groups. Discuss the podcast and answer these questions.

1 What are the main conclusions of the study?
2 Why do you think fit students get better grades?
3 Did you find the answers to the six questions you wrote in exercise 1?

RESEARCH References

1 **Read STUDY SKILL** Study the examples in the box. What information is included in each type of reference?

1 Book: *author, year, title, publishing house*
2 Newspaper: _____
3 Journal: _____
4 Website: _____

2 Rewrite the information so that it follows the referencing style in the Study Skill box. Identify each type of reference (book, website, etc.).

1 & / Geology Today / (2011) / Campbell, T / 14/2: 24–27. / Jurassic coast reveals more surprises / Hussain, A
2 Oxford / Gale, S. / OUP / Patterns in Pronunciation / (1997) / Fantoni, L / &
3 Kenyan Daily News / Tourism set to increase over five years / Odinga, J / (2010, January 23)

3 Work in groups. Discuss the questions.

1 Do you have difficulty in finding information on topics? How can you overcome this?
2 How can you be sure your sources are reliable?
3 When should you record any sources you may use? Do you have difficulty writing references? How can a computer help you?

4 Find information on another alternative therapy mentioned in the unit. Then write a reference.

STUDY SKILL Referencing

When you carry out research it is important to say where you found the information. This is one frequently used system, the APA system.

Book: Perez, V., & Thompson, L. (2009). *The Basics of Economics.* New York, Harper & Row.

Newspaper: Darwish, S. (1998, September 12). Natural gas production to rise. *Gulf Daily News.*

Journal or magazine article: Desai, V. (2005) Population trends in West Bengal. *International Development Journal,* 24/3: 48–59.

Website: Tykov, I. (2009). Breakthrough in photovoltaic cell design. Retrieved October 12, 2010 from: http://www.solarnews.com/mission/3498/features.htm

Different universities and different departments may use different systems.

SPEAKING Organizing a presentation

1 Work in groups and think about presentations you have seen in the past. Discuss these questions: What makes a good presenter? What makes a bad presenter? Use the diagrams to record your ideas.

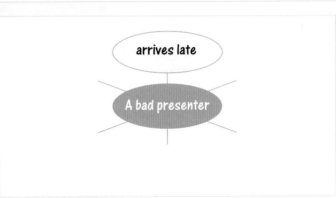

2 Look at the quotation below. It is common advice for people learning how to make a good presentation. What do you think it means? Discuss in small groups.

> **'Tell them what you are going to tell them. Tell them. Then tell them what you've told them.'**

3 [Read STUDY SKILL] 🔊 2.6 Listen to five excerpts from presentations. Decide if they come from the introduction (I), the main body (B) or the conclusion (C). Write I, B or C next to the numbers.

1 ___ 2 ___ 3 ___ 4 ___ 5 ___

4 Match the topics A–E with the presentation structure or headings 1–5.

A How to reduce road accidents

B Education in Japan and France

C Rising sea levels

D Changing methods of communication

E Tea production: from plantation to tea bag

1 ☐ past – present – future   4 ☐ compare and contrast
2 ☐ steps in a process   5 ☐ cause and effect
3 ☐ problem – solutions

STUDY SKILL
Presentations (1) Structure

Normally a presentation will contain:
- an introduction: Tell them what you are going to tell them.
- the body – main content: Tell them what you have to say.
- a conclusion: Tell them what you have told them.

Further divisions in the main body of the presentation can be made depending on the topic. For example, divisions by:
- time (chronology)
- causes and effects
- problems and solutions
- steps in a process

Introducing a presentation

1 Discuss the following questions in small groups.

1 What is the main aim of the introduction to a talk or presentation?

2 What information should it include?

2 **Read STUDY SKILL** 2.7 Listen to this introduction to a presentation on alternative therapies. As you listen, tick (✓) the sections of the talk that you hear in the table below.

☐ Introducing self (or others)　☐ Aim / Objective
☐ Title of presentation　　　　☐ Opinion
☐ Definitions　　　　　　　　☐ Plan
☐ Reasons

> **STUDY SKILL** Presentations (2) Introductions
>
> The introduction to a presentation includes:
> - a brief introduction of the presenter.
> - an explanation of the title of the presentation.
> - definitions of any terms.
> - reasons why the topic is important/interesting.
> - the aims/objectives.
> - the structure or plan of the talk.

3 Prepare a short introduction to a presentation on an alternative therapy. Use some of the information you collected in the Research task. Use the headings to plan your introduction. Use expressions from the Language Bank to help you.

| Title (Explain the title of the talk) |
| Definition (Explain any terms) |
| Reasons (Why did you choose this topic?) |
| Aims / Objectives (What do you aim to do?) |
| Plan (What is the structure of the talk?) |

> **LANGUAGE BANK** The language of introductions
>
> | | |
> |---|---|
> | Introducing self (or others): | *I'd like to introduce ...*
My name is ... / I am a ... / I work for ... |
> | Title: | *Today I'm going to talk about ... / I'd like to discuss ...* |
> | Definitions: | *Let me explain what I mean by ...*
... is usually defined as ... |
> | Reasons: | *... is an important / relevant issue nowadays.*
Why should we discuss ...? Well, I think ... |
> | Aim / Objective: | *My aim is to ...　What I want to do is ...* |
> | Opinion: | *I believe ... / I think ... / In my opinion ...* |
> | Plan: | *First I'll look at ...　Later I plan to ...*
Finally, I hope to ... |
> | Verbs: | *look at, describe, explain, examine, discuss, outline, talk about ...* |

4 Give your introduction to the class.

5 Briefly discuss the presentations. Did students cover the main points in their introductions? Were the introductions successful? Were you interested? Did you want to find out more about the topic?

VOCABULARY DEVELOPMENT Recording vocabulary

1 Read STUDY SKILL Look at one method of recording vocabulary below. How are the words organized? What information is given? Discuss with a partner.

English		Spanish
to keep	–	guardar
to kill	–	matar
kind	–	amiable
knife	–	el cuchillo
to know	–	saber
land	–	la tierra
language	–	la lengua

STUDY SKILL Recording vocabulary

It is important to make a record of new words. This helps you to:
- find the words quickly.
- review them.
- learn how to use them.

There are several methods of recording vocabulary including:
- a notebook.
- word cards.
- electronically.

In a notebook you can have all the words in one place. You can organize the words by topic, by grammatical form or alphabetically.

With word cards you can use both sides of the card and write different information on each.

2 Look at the example of a word card. It shows both sides of the card. What information is given on each side? What other information could you add? How would you use cards like these? Discuss your ideas with your partner.

evidence

/'evɪdəns/

part of speech	noun
collocations	to give, to find, to have – evidence, clear, conclusive, plenty of – evidence
word family	evident, evidently
definition	information tending to establish fact
example sentences	There is clear evidence of climate change. He gave evidence in the court.

3 Choose a verb, noun, and an adjective from the list below and design your own word cards. Use a dictionary to help.

Verb	to present, to rent, to practise
Noun	interview, report, lecture
Adjective	careful, intelligent, academic

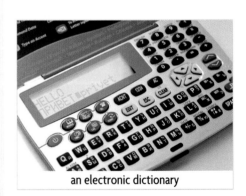

an electronic dictionary

4 Read STUDY SKILL Design a page for a vocabulary notebook. The topic is 'alternative medicine'. What vocabulary would you choose? What information would you include about these words? Add pictures and diagrams.

STUDY SKILL Using pictures and diagrams

Pictures and diagrams can help you remember a word, e.g.

stethoscope

REVIEW

1 🔊 **2.8** Listen to the discussion. What evidence do the speakers provide for the claims?

1 Students need a lot of energy to perform at university.
2 Most students do not have a healthy diet.

2 🔊 **2.8** Listen to the discussion again and match the speakers with their opinions.

1 Gemma   a There is no clear answer.
2 Phil   b Successful students need to eat healthily.
3 Roberta   c A healthy diet is not necessary for academic success.

3 🔊 **2.9** Listen to the lecturer and take notes about hydrotherapy, using the headings.

First used: _____

Reintroduced by (where / when): _____

Works by:

1 _____

2 _____

Treats: _____

4 Write references for items 1–2.

1

NUTRITION AND THE BRAIN

by Michael Kovak

© 1994

Allston College Press
Vermont, USA

2

http://www.healthyacademia.co.uk/articles/sugarvprotein/

Sugar v Protein:
How what we eat affects our performance

Shirley Reynolds M.D., May 23, 2007

5 Read the excerpts from a presentation. Discuss with a partner the order in which you think they would appear.

☐ 'The most obvious solution is to …'
☐ 'So, to summarize, we need to be aware of …'
☐ 'We realize that one of the biggest problems that we are facing is …'
☐ 'Hi. First a bit about myself– I'm Dr. Mark Sanchez from …'
☐ 'Today, I'm going to explain how conventional therapies and alternative therapies can be used together.'

6 Imagine you are going to give a presentation about staying healthy at university. With a partner, decide which information you are going to include in the introduction. Then practise your introductions.

3 Changing cities

LISTENING SKILLS Activating what you know • Critical thinking (3) Fact or opinion?
• Note-taking (2) Linear notes • Recognizing signposts
SPEAKING SKILLS Expressing opinions • Presentations (3) Organizing the main content
VOCABULARY DEVELOPMENT Academic words

LISTENING The history of a city

1 Work with a partner. Discuss these questions.

1 Look at the pictures. What do they show?
2 Why do people move to cities?
3 How do cities change to accommodate the people who move there?
4 Think of a city you know. How has it changed?

2 Look at these words which describe cities and city life. Which words are positive, which are negative and which are neutral?

> polluted   sophisticated   urban   sprawling   major
> bustling   industrial   congested   developing   filthy
> suburbs   capital   slums   overcrowded   cosmopolitan

London today

3 **Read STUDY SKILL** What do you know about London? Do the quiz below.

1 London was founded by …

   a the Vikings   **b** the French   **c** the Romans   **d** the Greeks

2 Which river passes through London?

   a the Thames   **b** the Severn   **c** the Hudson   **d** the Rhine

3 How much did the population grow in the 19th century?

   a by one million   **b** by two million   **c** by three million
   d by more than five million

4 The London Underground railway system is also called …

   a the Subway   **b** the Tube   **c** the Tunnel   **d** the Metro

5 What caused Parliament to close in the summer of 1858?

   a a fire   **b** a plague   **c** a war   **d** a bad smell

Life in 19th-century London slums

STUDY SKILL Activating what you know

A useful way to prepare for a topic is by discovering what you already know about it. Ask yourself:

■ What do I know about this topic?
■ What don't I know? What would I like to find out?

A busy street in the 19th century

4 Read the extract from a book review and answer the questions.

1 Who is Martin Holt?
2 What is his book about?
3 In Martin Holt's opinion, what do successful cities do?
4 What do you think the word 'infrastructure' means?

A horse-drawn omnibus

Urban Ideas

It seems that more and more people throughout the developing world want to live in cities. But what awaits these new migrants from rural areas? Many of them end up in slums, with little infrastructure or social support systems in place. In his new book, *Metropolis: The Challenges and Successes of Urbanism*, social historian Martin Holt explores this issue, with a keen sense of the history, examining the blossoming megacities of today, like Mumbai and Lagos, in relation to cities which have undergone similar transformations in the past, like Paris and London. Throughout the book he puts forward the argument that for cities to succeed, we must provide sufficient infrastructure and social support for the poorest workers, who often build the growing cities.

5 3.1 Listen to the podcast 'UK History Alive'. Check your answers to the quiz in exercise 3.

6 **Read STUDY SKILL** Read sentences 1–5. Which are opinions? Make changes so they are presented as opinions.

1 London is the ninth biggest city in the world.
2 Dubai is a successful city.
3 The centre of Moscow is too crowded.
4 Mumbai will be an important cultural centre in the 21st century.
5 Lagos is Nigeria's most prosperous city.

7 3.1 Listen to the interview again. What does Martin Holt say about the following topics? Complete the notes.

London
History
  • founded in 1st century
  • important medieval trade centre – location
  • Great Fire in 1666 – 80% of homes destroyed
Causes of population growth
  • _____
  • _____
Infrastructure improvements in 19th-century London
  • _____
  • _____
  • _____
Challenges of growth
  • getting people from their homes to jobs
  • _____
  • _____

8 Work in small groups. Think about growing cities today and answer the questions.

1 Which cities are growing rapidly today? Why do people want to move to these cities?
2 What challenges do growing cities face in the 21st century?
3 What improvements can be made in today's growing cities?

STUDY SKILL Critical thinking (3)
Fact or opinion?

It is important to be able to differentiate between a fact and an opinion.

- A fact is something generally known to be true. It may also be proved scientifically, for example:
  Mount Everest is the highest mountain in the world.

- An opinion is a view held by a person or a group of people, for example:
  I believe Mount Everest is the most difficult mountain to climb.

Eco-cities

1 Look at the city in the picture. What do you notice about it? Where do you think it is located?

2 Prepare for a lecture on 'Masdar City – a zero-carbon city' by reading the information below.
   1 Look at the words in bold. Work out the meaning from the context.
   2 Compare your ideas with your partner.

Masdar City master plan

Green cities

An **eco-city** is a city designed to reduce environmental impact. It is inhabited by people dedicated to the **minimization** of inputs of energy, water and food, and output of heat, waste and air pollution – CO_2, methane – and water pollution. A **sustainable** city can feed itself with **minimal** reliance on the surrounding area, and power itself with **renewable** sources of energy. The aim is to create the smallest possible ecological footprint, to produce the lowest quantity of pollution possible, and to use land efficiently.

A zero-carbon city is powered exclusively by renewable energy sources. To become a zero-carbon city, an established modern city must reduce **emissions** of greenhouse gases to zero and all practices that emit greenhouse gases must stop. In addition, renewable energy must become the sole source of energy. This **transition** includes decarbonizing electricity (increasing the importance of the sources of renewable electricity) and zero-emission transport.

3 **Read STUDY SKILL** 🎧 3.2 Listen to the first part of the lecture. Correct the **bold** words and phrases in the notes.

> Masdar City – an example of a zero-carbon city
>
> **Definitions:**
>
> 1 Eco-city = [1]**economically healthy, has a** [2]**big impact** on the environment
>
> 2 Zero-carbon city = [3]**produces very little pollution**
>
> **Background to Masdar City:**
>
> Location – [4]**The UK**
>
> Population – eventually 50,000
>
> Architects – Foster and Partners – from [5]**UAE**
>
> Cost – between [6]**£1 & 2 billion**

STUDY SKILL
Note-taking (2) Linear notes

A common way to take notes is linear notes. Linear notes progress down the page in a line and make use of headings and points, e.g.

Sources of energy:

1 Renewable sources, e.g.
   wind (in UK, Norway, etc.)
   solar (in dry, sunny climates)
   hydroelectric (in mountainous regions)
2 Non-renewable sources, e.g.
   coal (in the USA, China)
   gas (in Russia, Middle East)
   oil (Gulf states)

4 🔊 3.3 Listen to the second part of the lecture and complete the notes for the headings.

> Sources of energy:
> 1 _____
> 2 _____
> Cooling of the city – by:
> 1 _____
> 2 _____
> 3 _____
> Transport in Masdar City:
> 1 _____
> 2 _____
> Future: _____

5 Check your notes with other students. Add further information to your notes if you can.

6 **Read STUDY SKILL** 🔊 3.4 Listen to extracts from the lecture again. Write the signposts that the lecturer uses as each new section of the talk is introduced.

Introduction: Today I'd like to talk about a very interesting urban development project – a new city called Masdar City.

Definitions:	_____	definitions. An eco-city …
Background:	_____	Masdar City itself. It's being …
Energy:	_____	energy? We've already …
Cooling:	_____	the cooling of the city.
	1 _____	is the design of the city …
	2 _____	, the walls will be covered with …
	3 _____	wind towers. These are traditional …
Transport:	_____	transport? How will the inhabitants …
Future:	_____	the future? Well, the city is due …

STUDY SKILL Recognizing signposts

Signposts are words and phrases that the lecturer uses to indicate the next part of the lecture – or a change in direction, for example:

First, second, then, next, finally …
I'd like to begin by …
Now let us move on to …
A further point is …
Now let's consider the question of …
Which leads me on to …

A speaker may use a question to introduce a new point, for example:

Now what about …?

Signposts show us the structure of the lecture and help us to follow what the lecturer says.

---

7 Use your notes in exercises 3 and 4 to review the talk. Work in small groups and give an oral summary of the talk, using your own words.

Interior View of Courtyard Building

Centre Courtyard and wind tower at the Masdar Institute

Personal Rapid Transit Station at Masdar Institute

SPEAKING Expressing opinions

1 Look at the photo of Zurich in Switzerland.

  1 What kind of place do you think it is?
  2 Would you like to live in this city?
  3 Why? / Why not? Discuss with a partner.

2 Several organizations make lists of the worlds'
best cities to live in. Study the list below and
decide which factors you think are important for
making a selection. Give reasons for your choices.

factor	ranking	reason
Climate		
Public transport		
Personal safety		
Education		
Health care		
Recreation		
Culture		
Political / Economic stability		

3 **Read STUDY SKILL** 🔊 3.5 Listen to an extract from a discussion between three
speakers, Carlos, Suzi and Peter. They are discussing the list of factors above.
Answer the questions.

  1 Which speaker wants climate to be at the top of the list?
  2 Which speaker is more worried about personal safety?
  3 What does Peter want at the top of the list?
  4 Which speakers express their views most reasonably?
  5 Which speaker do you think is less reasonable?

4 Work in small groups. Using the expressions in the Language Bank, discuss
the factors listed in exercise 2 and decide which are the most important and
which are the least important. Rank them 1–8. Give reasons for your choices.
For example:

factor	ranking	reason
Climate	*2*	*A pleasant climate is very important for people's happiness and health.*

LANGUAGE BANK The language of opinion

Expressing opinions	**Expressing a strong opinion**	**Expressing a cautious view**
As I see it / In my opinion ...	*I firmly / I really believe that ...*	*I think climate is probably the*
As far as I'm concerned ...	*I'm convinced that ...*	*most important factor ...*
Personally, I take the view that ...	*It is possible that ...*	
I think there is a good case for ... (-ing)	*I take your point / I see your point ... but I still believe ...*	

5 One member of each group should give a short summary of the discussion to
the rest of the class. Explain your rankings.

Organizing content

1 Look at the city in the picture with a partner. Describe its appearance and the facilities that it might have. Will cities like this be possible in the future? Why? / Why not?

2 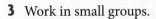 3.6 Listen to this short extract from a presentation on a city and answer the questions.
1 Which city is mentioned?
2 Which two factors are discussed?
3 Which three months are the hottest? Which month is the wettest?
4 What language is used to signal the introduction of the two topics?

3 Work in small groups.
1 Choose a city (not your own) that you would like to live in.
2 Find out information about the factors you discussed on page 24.

4 **Read STUDY SKILL** Organize your notes and prepare your presentation. Divide the presentation between members of the group.
1 Decide on the structure of your presentation.
2 Use a plan like the one below to help you.
3 Remember to include signposts.

factor	notes
Climate	
Public transport	
Personal safety	
Education	
Health care	
Recreation	
Culture	
Political / Economic stability	

5 In groups, give your presentation to the class. Use the expressions in the Language Bank. The rest of the class should take notes and ask questions.

6 Discuss all of the presentations.
1 How well were they organized?
2 Did they use signposts?
3 If they used the signposts, did these help you to follow the talk?

STUDY SKILL Presentations (3)
Organizing the main content

The main part of the talk is usually divided into a number of different sections. These may be:
- steps in a process
- stages in history
- issues
- causes / results
- a problem and solutions

It is important to organize the body of the talk and to signal each new part.

LANGUAGE BANK
Signalling stages and changes

Showing sequence:
- *first, second, then, next, after that, finally …*

Moving to another point:
- *Now let us move on to …*
- *A further point is …*
- *I'd like to look at …*
- *Let's turn to the question of … Now what about …?*

VOCABULARY DEVELOPMENT Learning academic vocabulary

1 **Read STUDY SKILL** Match the academic words on the left with the general words on the right.

academic	general
1 ☐ context	a possible
2 ☐ decline	b get
3 ☐ receive	c become worse
4 ☐ feasible	d basic services
5 ☐ innovative	e situation
6 ☐ infrastructure	f new
7 ☐ deteriorate	g fall

2 Use the academic words above to complete these sentences.

1 Despite the difficulties, the report said the project was _____ . As a result, the government decided to go ahead with it.

2 He was recruited because of his _____ thinking. The company liked his fresh, new ideas on marketing.

3 During the war the country's _____ was completely destroyed. Roads, bridges and communications had to be rebuilt.

4 There has been a slow _____ in the sale of books in recent years. This could be due to the effect of the Internet.

5 It is difficult to explain Tom's strange behaviour when we don't know the _____ .

6 Because of a rise in oil prices, oil-producing countries will _____ a huge increase in profits next year.

7 Repairs to the building must be carried out immediately. The whole structure of the building is beginning to _____ .

3 Read the introduction to a talk. Replace the general vocabulary in **bold** with the academic words in the box. Use a dictionary to help.

divide   define   sufficient   assisted   section   discuss   examine   pose

Good morning. Today I want to **talk about** / _____ [1] the problem of urban sprawl in countries in the developing world. I'm going to **split** / _____ [2] the talk into three parts.
The first **bit** / _____ [3] will be a short overview of the history of the problem over the last few hundred years.
Then I want to **look at** / _____ [4] the role of transport, in particular car ownership, and how this has **helped** / _____ [5] the spread of population away from city centres.
Thirdly, I'll focus on the role of government policy. I'll want to **ask** / _____ [6] the question – have governments given **enough** / _____ [7] attention to this problem?
But first of all I'd like to **give the meaning of** / _____ [8] the phrase 'urban sprawl'.

STUDY SKILL Academic words

Vocabulary can be divided into general and academic.

- **General words** are words in everyday use, e.g. *house, build, chat.*
- **Academic words** often come from Latin or Greek origins. They can be divided into general academic words and technical words.
- **General academic words** are commonly used in academic texts, formal lectures and discussions, e.g. *data, derived, theory.*
- **Technical words** are usually restricted to a particular field of study, e.g. *cathode* (electronics), *urbanist* (urban planning), *renal* (medicine).

An important resource is the Academic Word List, which is a list of the most common words in academic texts. You can find examples on the Internet.

context

innovative

REVIEW

1 🔊 **3.7** Listen to the speaker and put the sentences in the order you hear them. Then say if they are facts (F) or opinions (O).

1 Traffic congestion costs the economy money. ☐ ___
2 There is too much traffic in cities. ☐ ___
3 You have to pay to drive in the centre of London. ☐ ___
4 Urban planners are trying to design car-free cities. ☐ ___
5 More than 50% of people live in urban centres. ☐ ___
6 Being stuck in traffic is annoying. ☐ ___

2 🔊 **3.8** Listen to the talk about urban improvements in London. Complete the linear notes from the prompts.

> Topic:
>
> Transport history:
>
> Improvements:
>
>
>
> Parks history:
>
> Improvements:

A pedestrianized street

3 Use your notes to discuss the questions with a partner.

1 What are some of the problems with London's Underground?
2 What is being done to solve these problems?
3 Why has London got so many parks?
4 What improvements are being made to the parks today?
5 How do you think the improvements to the Underground and parks will benefit the people of London?

4 With a partner, discuss your opinions on the following topics.

1 Overcrowding in cities
2 The best place in the world to live
3 Affordable housing

5 Choose one of the topics in exercise 4. Discuss with your partner how you would organize a presentation on this topic. Then discuss what signposting language you would use in your presentation. Write five example sentences.

6 Use the academic words in the box to replace one word in each sentence.

> data   sector   strategies   transformation   obtained

1 Channel 7 news received a report critical of the architecture firm.
2 There has been a very dramatic change in the way cities raise money for public art.
3 The city council must develop better plans to conserve historic buildings.
4 The information from the survey is very clear.
5 The public part of the economy is operated by the government.

4 Issues in agriculture

LISTENING SKILLS Recognizing causes and solutions • References to earlier comments
• Listening to an illustrated talk
SPEAKING SKILLS Critical thinking (4) Seeing a problem from all sides • Pronunciation: numbers
• Presentations (4) Describing facts and figures
VOCABULARY DEVELOPMENT Collocations

LISTENING Feed the world

1 Look at the photos of two fields of maize above. Discuss the questions with your partner.

   1 What are the differences between the fields?
   2 What are the possible reasons for this?
   3 What crops are grown in your country?
   4 Does your country import food from other countries?

2 Which of these words and phrases would you associate with each picture? Write A or B.

   1 healthy crop of maize **B**   6 use of fertilizers ___
   2 poor quality soil ___   7 good harvest ___
   3 lack of water supply ___   8 seasonal drought ___
   4 irrigation system ___   9 dying plants ___
   5 high quality seed ___   10 low productivity ___

3 Read the radio programme notes below. Check any new vocabulary. Discuss the questions in small groups.

> **GLOBAL VIEW Panel discussion**
>
> Food riots have taken place in several countries of the world. Rising food prices for basic foods such as wheat, rice, and maize, have meant that many families in developing countries are going hungry. In addition, climate change is resulting in droughts in some parts of the world and floods in others. Rising energy costs have also played a part. Does this mean that the world is heading for an economic crisis? Today's panel looks at the global food crisis – its causes and possible solutions.

   1 What is the discussion going to be about?
   2 What do you think are the causes of this problem worldwide?
   3 What are the possible solutions to this problem?
   4 How can we produce enough food for the world's population?

4 **Read STUDY SKILL** 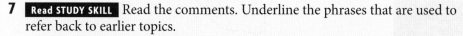 4.1 Listen to the first part of the panel discussion and take notes on the causes of the crisis.

Biofuels

STUDY SKILL Recognizing causes and solutions

Signal words help us follow causes and solutions to a problem, for example:

Causes:

- *What are the causes of …?*
- *I think there are a number of causes …*
- *What other factors are there …?*

Solutions:

- *What can we do to solve this problem?*
- *Another simple solution would be to …*
- *One thing we could do is …*

---

5 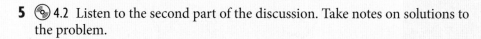 4.2 Listen to the second part of the discussion. Take notes on solutions to the problem.

6 Use your notes from exercises 4 and 5 to discuss the following questions with a partner.

1 Why aren't farmers producing enough food?
2 Why are biofuels described as a 'disaster'?
3 What does the speaker mean by making crops 'weather-proof'?
4 What did the government do in Malawi? Why was this more effective than importing food to the country?

7 **Read STUDY SKILL** Read the comments. Underline the phrases that are used to refer back to earlier topics.

1 As I said earlier, wheat production is declining in some parts of the world.
2 I'd just like to reiterate that I think this is a global problem.
3 Before we go on I'd just like to come back to what Tom said about energy costs.
4 I think Laura made a good point about environmental factors, but I'd like to add something.

STUDY SKILL
References to earlier comments

In a discussion involving several people, speakers often refer back to things said earlier in the discussion, for example:

As I mentioned a moment ago, biofuels are not the answer.

8 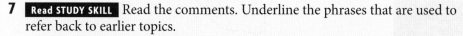 4.2 Read the phrases in the table. The speakers use these phrases to refer back to what they said earlier. Listen to the second part of the discussion again. Match the phrases with the topics they are referring to.

phrase		topic	
1 ☐ I'd like to come back to what I said earlier		a	seeds, fertilizers and water for farmers
2 ☐ I mentioned earlier		b	low productivity
3 ☐ But let's go back to the first point we made		c	climate change and drought
4 ☐ Yes, there are – as I said at the beginning of our discussion		d	biofuels

9 Look at the three solutions that the speakers mention in exercise 5 again. Work in small groups and evaluate these solutions.

1 How effective is each of the solutions?
2 What possible difficulties are there with these solutions?
3 Can you think of other solutions that the speakers did not mention?
4 Which solution is probably the most effective?

Malawi – a success story

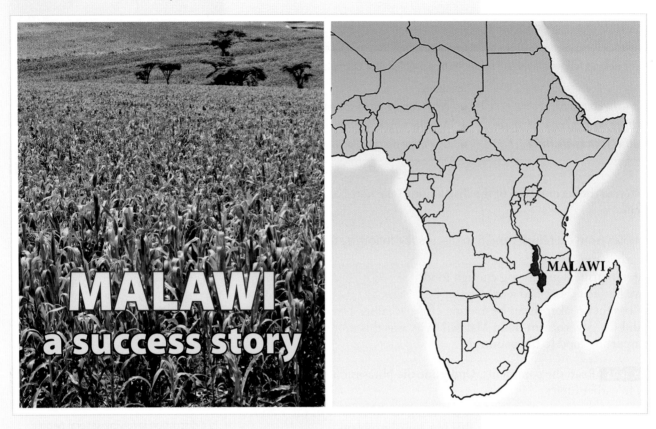

MALAWI a success story

MALAWI

1 You are going to listen to an illustrated talk on food production in the African country Malawi. In small groups brainstorm what you know about Malawi. Include the following:

| location | size | capital city | population | main exports | climate |

2 🔊 4.3 Listen to the introduction. What is the main aim of the talk?
☐ To discuss the causes of and solutions to the global food crisis.
☐ To explain the food crisis and the role of international agencies.
☐ To show how small, local projects can help to solve the global food crisis.
☐ To describe Malawi and the different types of agriculture in the country.

3 **Read STUDY SKILL** 🔊 4.4 Listen to the main part of the talk. Complete the handout below with facts and figures about Malawi. Check your answers with a partner.

MALAWI – FACTS AND FIGURES

Location: _____

Population: _____

Capital city: _____

Area sq km: _____

Life expectancy: _____

Climate: _____

Main or staple crop: _____

STUDY SKILL
Listening to an illustrated talk

It is important for listeners to understand how slides in the presentation relate to what the speaker is saying.

To draw your attention to the slides, a speaker will use phrases such as:
■ *Let me begin by showing you …*
■ *Now if we look at … we can see that …*
■ *This graph / chart / table indicates …*
■ *And here you can see …*

4 🎧 4.5 Listen to the rest of the talk on Malawi. Match the slides with titles 1–6.

1 What the world should do
2 Problems facing farmers in Malawi
3 What farmers need
4 Maize production (metric tonnes)
5 The importance of irrigation
6 Three harvests a year

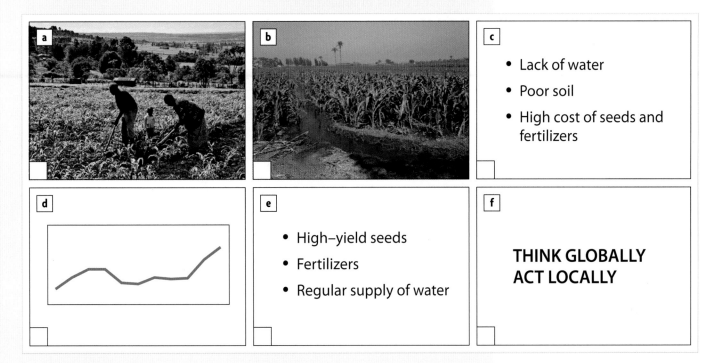

c
- Lack of water
- Poor soil
- High cost of seeds and fertilizers

e
- High–yield seeds
- Fertilizers
- Regular supply of water

f

THINK GLOBALLY ACT LOCALLY

5 🎧 4.6 Listen to the speaker describing the graph of maize production. Complete the graph below with the information for the missing years.

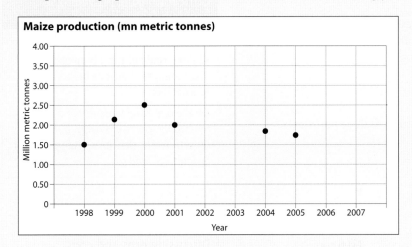

6 Work in small groups. Discuss the Malawi solution.

1 What were the main actions the Malawi government took?
2 How did the use of irrigation help farmers?
3 Is the Malawi model a good solution for other countries? What problems could there be?

SPEAKING   Discussing pros and cons

1 🔊 4.7 Listen to this short talk on biofuels and answer the questions.

  1 What are biofuels?
  2 What are the two main types of biofuel? What are they produced from?
  3 Which countries are the main users of biofuels?
  4 What are biofuels mainly used for?
  5 How are the crops converted to biofuel? Complete the simple flow chart
    below to describe the process. Label the chart with the phrases in the box.

| biofuel sold | fuel distributed | transported to bio-refinery | crops harvested | converted to ethanol |

2 **Read STUDY SKILL** List the advantages and disadvantages of biofuels. Discuss
with a partner and give reasons for your answers.

3 🔊 4.8 Listen to this discussion between three students, Samira, Mike and
Hiroto. Decide which student:

  1 is generally in favour of biofuels.
  2 is generally against.
  3 is neutral – can see both sides.

4 You are going to discuss the pros and cons of biofuels. Before you start:
  1 Decide on your roles:

A	B	C
In Favour	**Against**	**Neutral**
Main points:	Main points:	Main points:
Evidence:	Evidence:	Evidence:

  2 Prepare your role. What are your main points? What evidence do you
    have to support those points? Make some notes.
  3 Discuss the topic in groups of three, one A, one B, and one C, using the
    expressions in the Language Bank.

5 One person from each group should summarize the discussion for the rest of
the class. What did you decide?

STUDY SKILL
Critical thinking (4) Seeing a
problem from all sides

It is important to see a problem from
all sides. Find out the advantages and
disadvantages of an idea before coming
to a decision:

*On the one hand biofuels are a cheap,
renewable source of energy, but
unfortunately, they also take up a lot of
agricultural land so …*

LANGUAGE BANK
Discussing pros and cons

In favour:
  One advantage is …
  A clear benefit of … is …
  I think … outweighs the negative points.

Against:
  … has to be seen as a disadvantage.
  I think there is a strong case against …

Neutral:
  *On the one hand … but on the other
    hand …*

Presenting facts and figures

1 **Read STUDY SKILL** ⊚ 4.9 Listen and write the numbers you hear. Then practise saying the numbers out loud in pairs.

1 _____
2 _____
3 _____
4 _____
5 _____
6 _____

> **STUDY SKILL** Pronunciation: numbers
>
> It is important to be able to say or read numbers clearly in a presentation.
>
> *307,451 – three hundred and seven thousand, four hundred and fifty-one*
>
> *12,239,007 – twelve million, two hundred and thirty-nine thousand and seven*
>
> *82% – eighty-two per cent*
>
> *39.65 – thirty-nine point six five*
>
> *0.159 – zero (nought) point one five nine*
>
> *¼ – one quarter*

2 ⊚ 4.10 Listen to this short presentation on a North African country. As you listen, take notes using the headings. You should write down all of the facts and figures you are given.

> Country
> Location
> Area sq km
> Population
> Climate
> Life expectancy
> Main crops

3 **Read STUDY SKILL** Work in groups of three. Each member should choose *one* of the countries below. Use the information to prepare a short talk on the country using the expressions in the Language Bank.

Country	Laos	Peru	Lesotho
Location	SE Asia – Thailand / Vietnam	S America – Chile / Ecuador	Africa – surrounded by South Africa
Area sq km	236,000	1,285,220	30,555
Population	6,368,000	28,303,000	2,022,000
Climate	wet monsoon (May–November), dry season (December–April)	tropical in east, dry desert in west	cool, dry winters, hot, wet summers
Life expectancy	55.5	69.8	34.4
Main crops produced (metric tonnes per annum)	Rice 2,350,000, Vegetables 660,000, Sweet potatoes 248,000	Sugar cane 7,100,000, Potatoes 3,200,000, Rice 2,350,000	Maize 150,000, Potatoes 90,000, Wheat 51,000

> **STUDY SKILL** Presentations (4) Describing facts and figures
>
> When you describe data, make sure you:
> - use visuals where possible to help the listeners understand the data.
> - pronounce the numbers, fractions, etc. clearly.
> - repeat the information if necessary.
> - select only the important or relevant information.
>
> It is not always necessary to give the listeners every item of information or every result.

LANGUAGE BANK
Language to describe facts and figures

Some of the language needed to describe data about a country:

Location: *It's located in …; It borders … and …; It lies between … and …*

Area: *The area is …; It covers an area of … square kilometres*

Climate: *It's wet in winter; It's tropical in the south.*

Population: *The population is …; It has a population of …*

Life expectancy: *It has a life expectancy of … years; The life expectancy is high / low.*

Main crops: *The main crops are …; Production was … metric tonnes.*

4 Give a short talk on the country you selected to your group. The other members should close their books and take notes while listening to the talk. They should use the headings in the first column in the table in exercise 3 for the notes.

VOCABULARY DEVELOPMENT Collocations

1 Read STUDY SKILL Complete the table with suitable verbs that form collocations with the table headings. Use a dictionary or information from the unit to help you.

a problem	a solution	a conclusion	a discussion	crops
face				

STUDY SKILL Collocations

It is important to learn which words collocate with one another. For example, the noun *discussion* collocates with the following verbs:

have, hold, enter into, be involved in, take part in, generate, participate in, etc.

and the following adjectives:

brief, full, frank, detailed, long, serious, preliminary, bilateral, etc.

It also collocates with nouns:
group –, – document
and prepositions
– about, – between.

Collocation dictionaries can help you.

2 Write sentences using the prompts below and the correct form of verbs from the table in exercise 1.

1 Malawi/problem/lack of water
2 Scientists/solution/global warming
3 The meeting/conclusion
4 The staff/discussion/salaries
5 Malawi/crops/maize and tea

3 Complete these sentences using a collocation with *crisis*. Use words from the collocation dictionary entry below.

1 There will be a _____ economic crisis in the near future if we cannot find alternatives to fossil fuels.

2 The drought last year _____ a crisis for the government as food supplies were insufficient for the needs of the people.

3 Many seabirds were killed _____ the oil crisis in the Gulf of Mexico in 2010.

4 Relations between the president and the prime minister reached crisis _____ after the president's comments to the newspapers.

5 Sonia suffered a crisis of _____ after she saw that her examination grades were poor.

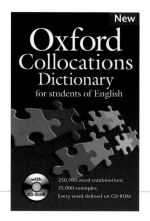

New
Oxford
Collocations
Dictionary
for students of English

250,000 word combinations
75,000 examples
Every word defined on CD-ROM

---

crisis *noun*

ADJ. acute, grave, major, serious, severe, terrible | growing, mounting | impending, looming | international | constitutional, economic, financial, fiscal, political | cash, debt, energy, hostage, housing, oil | family, personal | identity | mid-life

VERB + CRISIS be faced with, be hit by, face, go through, have *(informal)*, suffer. *The British coal industry is facing a serious crisis. He's having a mid-life crisis.* | cause, create, lead to, precipitate, provoke, spark off | deal with, defuse, ease, handle, overcome, resolve, respond to, solve, tackle *Union leaders are taking immediate steps to defuse the crisis.* | survive, weather | avert, prevent | aggravate

CRISIS + VERB arise *waiting for the next crisis to arise* | deepen, worsen

PREP. during a/the ~ *Three people died during the hostage crisis.* | in (a/the) – *The government is in crisis.*

CRISIS + NOUN point *The team's dismal season has reached crisis point.*

PHRASES a crisis of confidence *The company is suffering a severe crisis of confidence.*

REVIEW

1 🔊 4.11 Listen to the excerpt from a presentation and answer the questions.

1 What is the 'water crisis'?
2 What is one of the causes of the 'water crisis'?
3 What solution does the speaker suggest?

2 🔊 4.11 Listen again and choose which two slides below should be used with this presentation.

1 **Water pollution** • industry • agriculture • poor city planning	**2** **Water crisis** 1.1 billion people lack access to clean water.
3 Trees' roots store water underground	**4** **Deforestation** • Loss of animal habitats • Pollution • Climate change

3 What are the advantages and disadvantages of each of the topics listed below? Complete the table with your ideas and give reasons.

topic	advantages	reasons	disadvantages	reasons
aiding poor countries				
wind farms				
studying overseas				

4 Discuss the topics in exercise 3 with a partner.

5 Global culture

LISTENING SKILLS Listening for questions • Critical thinking (5) Anecdotal evidence
  • Recognizing what information is important
SPEAKING SKILLS Conducting interviews • Presenting with graphics
VOCABULARY DEVELOPMENT Suffixes

LISTENING Are we all becoming the same?

1 Read the possible definitions of the word 'culture'. What does 'culture' mean to you? Discuss the question in small groups.

Paintings, music, literature, theatre ...

The beliefs and values held by a group.

The way a group of people live or behave.

2 Do the *How global are you?* quiz. Answer *Yes* or *No*. Then calculate your score.

> ### HOW GLOBAL ARE YOU?
>
> | | |
> |---|---|
> | 1 Do you eat sushi? | Y/N |
> | 2 Do you regularly watch foreign TV shows such as 'House'? | Y/N |
> | 3 Do you like to watch international sports events like the Olympics? | Y/N |
> | 4 Have you seen a Bollywood film? | Y/N |
> | 5 Do you wear jeans? | Y/N |
> | 6 Have you ever visited a Starbucks coffee shop? | Y/N |
> | 7 Have you heard of the footballer Lionel Messi? | Y/N |
> | 8 Do you use social networking sites such as Facebook? | Y/N |
> | 9 Do you have a mobile phone? | Y/N |
> | 10 Do you know why Jimmy Choo is famous? | Y/N |
>
> **KEY:** If you answered **Yes**:
>
> 9–10 times: It seems you are very global in your outlook.
>
> 4–8 times: You are somewhere between your local culture and global culture.
>
> 0–3 times: You are probably strongly connected to your national or local culture.

3 Discuss the following questions in small groups.
  1 What do you think 'global culture' means? Give some examples.
  2 Are we moving towards a global culture? If we are, does this really mean we are all becoming the same?
  3 What are possible advantages and disadvantages of the globalization of culture? Make notes.

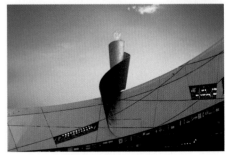

4 Read this introduction to a paper on global culture. Discuss these questions with your partner.

1 What do you think is meant by the terms 'cultural boundaries', 'Western ideals' and 'sense of community'?

2 What are the two possible outcomes of global culture that are mentioned?

The Globalization of Culture

Technology has now created the possibility of a global culture. The Internet, satellites, and cable TV are sweeping away <u>cultural boundaries</u>. Global entertainment companies shape the dreams of ordinary citizens, wherever they live. This spread of values, norms, and culture tends to promote <u>Western ideals</u>. Will local cultures inevitably fall victim to this global "consumer" culture? Will global products – food, fashion and entertainment mean the end of local production? Will English replace all other languages? In other words, will consumer values destroy peoples' <u>sense of community</u>? Or, on the contrary, will a common culture lead the way to greater shared values and political unity?

5 **Read STUDY SKILL** 5.1 Listen to a discussion between four students. They have just read the article on The Globalization of Culture above and are expressing their views. Complete the questions that the speakers ask.

1 JANE: ... Firstly, to what extent is globalization of culture actually happening? Lee, _____?

2 LEE: ... There are still many areas of the world that have kept their own culture. China, for example. _____? Miriam?

3 SUNIL: ... And I think the result of that can be the suppression of local culture. Lee, _____?

4 JANE: ... Or does it mean that local cultures will disappear? _____?

5 JANE: I think I agree with Miriam on this. The world will become less interesting. Sunil, _____?

STUDY SKILL
Listening for questions

Listening for questions can be very helpful for following a discussion. This is especially useful if you are listening to a recorded discussion such as a podcast or a radio programme.

Questions can help you follow the topic:
What do other people think about these trade policies?

They can also help you know who will speak next:
What do you think, Andy?

6 5.1 Listen to the discussion again and match the speakers with the views.

1 Jane	a Local cultures are still strong.
2 Lee	b The media exaggerate the importance of global culture.
3 Miriam	c Some foods are popular all over the world.
4 Sunil	d 'Cultural boundaries' have disappeared.
	e Global food companies suppress local culture.
	f Globalization makes travel less interesting.
	g Globalization means you have things in common with people in other countries.

7 5.2 Listen to part of the discussion again. What are each of the participant's views on the globalization of culture? Are they in favour of it, against it or neutral?

8 **Read STUDY SKILL** 5.3 Listen to excerpts from the discussion. Decide whether the evidence they give on each topic is anecdotal or factual.

| fashion – designer labels | the TV programme *House* |
| Pizza Hut   Russian food | the film *Avatar* |

9 Compare your answers with a partner. How could the anecdotal evidence be made stronger? What factual evidence could the speakers provide?

STUDY SKILL
Critical thinking (5) Anecdotal evidence

Anecdotal evidence is based on an event that happened to the participant or someone they know, for example:
Bollywood DVDs are popular in the UK. When I was in London, I saw several shops that sold them.

It may be relevant in some cases but it is generally less useful than 'factual evidence' or 'scientific evidence'.

Coffee and culture

1 Discuss the questions in groups.

1 Why are coffee shop chains so popular in many countries?
2 Are they a good thing? What are the arguments for and against global chains like these?

2 You are going to listen to a lecture entitled 'Global companies'. Tick (✓) the topics the talk will cover. Choose from the list.

Global companies

☐ Global marketing
☐ Advantages of going global
☐ World population growth
☐ The problems of international airlines
☐ International brands
☐ Exports from China
☐ The growth of global companies

3 Read the three lecture titles on the right. Choose one that interests you.

1 Predict the content of the lecture.
2 Write five questions you think the lecturer will examine.

| Sushi – the new international food |
| English as a global language |
| Jeans – the world's most popular clothing |

4 You are going to listen to a lecture on the history of Starbucks, the global coffee house. Write down five questions you think the lecturer will address.

5 🔊 5.4 Listen to the lecture. Check if your questions were answered.

6 **Read STUDY SKILL** 🔊 5.5 Now listen to the introduction to the lecture again. How does the speaker show that the following words and phrases are important?

1 global village
2 history of Starbucks
3 implications of this expansion

STUDY SKILL Recognizing what information is important

When taking notes, it is essential to recognize what information is important. Listen for any clues that the speaker may give. For example, the speaker may:

- speak more slowly and clearly (with special emphasis).
- pause before a word, phrase or number.
- repeat a word, phrase or number.
- focus on specific facts and figures when discussing a slide.
- spell, rephrase or give definitions of any unusual or difficult words or names.
- use signals, such as 'Here is the problem ...' or 'What does this tell us?'
- simply say: 'You may want to write this down.' or 'This is important!'

Make sure you can recognize and write down quickly:

- large numbers, decimals, percentages, fractions

---

7 🔊 **5.6** Now listen to the next part of the lecture. Listen for important information and complete the 'History' section of the handout below. Compare your answers with your partner.

Starbucks: a Global Company

Structure of lecture:

1 History

2 Current situation

3 Implications / what does it all mean?

1 History

YEAR

__1971_____ Starbucks founded – in US city of ¹_____

²_____ Howard ³_____ joined company

⁴_____ first stores outside Seattle – all across ⁵_____

⁶_____ first Starbucks outside North America – in ⁷_____

⁸_____ Starbucks entered ⁹_____ market

By ¹⁰_____ more than ¹¹_____ outlets worldwide

Between ¹²_____ and ¹³_____ Starbucks opened ¹⁴_____ stores every year

8 🔊 **5.7** Listen to the last part of the lecture. Write notes for the prompts in the final sections of the handout, 'Situation today' and 'Implications'.

9 Use your notes from exercise 8 to answer these questions. Check your answers with a partner.

1 How many Starbucks stores are there now? In how many countries?
2 How many stores will there be in the future?
3 Which country is second to the USA in the number of outlets?
4 According to the website, what does Starbucks offer customers?
5 Why are some people against Starbucks? Give two reasons.
6 According to supporters of Starbucks, what do people want?
7 What does being a 'global brand' mean for the customer?

10 Discuss the following questions in small groups.

1 What did you learn from the talk?
2 Did you change your views on global companies such as Starbucks?
3 What do you think is the main advantage of Starbucks, and the main disadvantage?
4 Think about other global companies you know. How are they the same as (or different from) Starbucks?

2 Situation today

Stores (How many? / Where?):

Plans for future:

Largest markets:

3 Implications

Website:

Opponents say:

Supporters say:

SPEAKING Conducting an interview

1 Discuss your shopping habits with a partner. Answer these questions.

  1 Do you shop online? Why / Why not?
  2 Do you usually buy local products or international brands? Why / Why not?
  3 How important is price when you go shopping?
  4 Do you shop in supermarkets or traditional markets? Why / Why not?
  5 Do you look for Fairtrade products? If you do, what do you buy?

A traditional market

2 Look at the survey questions 1–4 below. Match them with the question types in the box:

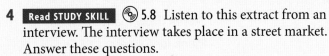

| multiple choice | Yes / No | rating questions | open questions |

  1 What are the advantages of shopping in malls?
  2 Do you use online shopping?
  3 Where do you usually shop for food? In:
     a a supermarket **b** a street market **c** local stores **d** other
  4 How important is the price of a product when you are shopping?
     a very important **b** important **c** not very important
     d unimportant

3 Discuss the four question types in pairs.

  1 Which types are closed questions?
  2 Which questions give the researcher the most information?
  3 Which questions are the most difficult to write?
  4 For which types of question is it easiest to collect the results?

4 **Read STUDY SKILL** 🎧 5.8 Listen to this extract from an interview. The interview takes place in a street market. Answer these questions.

  1 Does the interviewer explain the purpose of the survey?
  2 Are all the questions 'closed questions'?
  3 Does the interviewer include a Yes / No question?
  4 Does the interviewee ask questions for clarification?

5 You are going to conduct interviews in order to collect data on shopping habits. Prepare questions to ask related to the five topics in exercise 1. Use a range of question types.

6 Test your questions with your partner. Record the answers to see how clear the information is. Make changes to your questions if necessary.

7 Choose your survey participants and conduct the interviews. Follow these steps:

  • Introduce yourself and explain the purpose of the interview.
  • Ask your questions. Clarify the questions if necessary.
  • Make a note of the answers.
  • Compile the results.

STUDY SKILL Conducting interviews

Before the interview:

■ decide on the group of people you need to interview for your study.
■ prepare your questions in advance and learn them.
■ design the questions to get the information you need expressed clearly.

Remember:

■ closed questions (Yes / No, multiple choice, etc.) give you more facts for your analysis.
■ open questions (*What do you think of …?*) are more difficult to analyse.
■ You may want to add factual information such as gender and age group.

During the interview:

■ introduce yourself politely and explain the purpose of the interview.
■ ask the person if they would mind answering some questions.
■ ask the questions and get clarification if necessary.
■ keep a clear record of the answers.

Presenting results

1 How important are the following factors when presenting results visually? Discuss with a partner and put them in order of importance (1–4).

☐ All of your results are shown in the graphics.
☐ Attractive ways of displaying the data are used.
☐ Each graphic is given a relevant title.
☐ The most important information is presented clearly.

2 **Read STUDY SKILL** You are going to prepare graphics to show the results of your survey. Follow the steps:

- Decide what information from your survey you want to present.
- Decide which type of graphics will work best for that information.
- Draw your graphics on paper or create them using a computer.
- Remember to label your graphics and give them titles.

3 5.9 Listen to the interviewer explaining his results on the street market survey. Complete the graphics with the following information:

STUDY SKILL
Presenting with graphics

Data from interviews can be presented using graphics such as:
- pie charts
- bar charts
- tables

When you refer to data in the form of graphics, you should look for information that is important:
- pick out high values or low values.
- pick out surprising or interesting data.
- look for trends when you can.
- do not read out all of the information in a table.

1 Complete the labels in the pie chart: a) *outside*, b) *Manchester*.

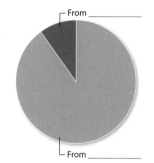

3 Draw the bars in the chart.

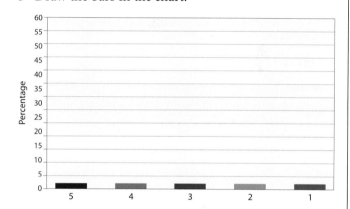

2 Label the bar chart: a) *weekly*, b) *daily*.

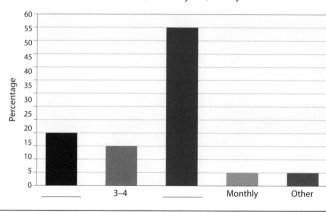

4 Complete the table with the following labels: *car*, *bus*, *walking*, and *other*.

Day	1_____	2_____	3_____	4_____
Wednesday	56%	10%	31%	3%
Saturday	34%	11%	47%	8%

4 Using the graphics you prepared, explain the results of your survey to the rest of the class with expressions from the Language Bank.

LANGUAGE BANK Language for graphics

Referring to the visual:

You can see from the pie chart / table / bar chart …
This pie chart / table / bar chart shows …
It can be seen from this chart / table / bar chart …
If you look at … you can see …

Describing the data:

The overall trend is …
The majority / Most of …
A large number / percentage of … / The largest number / percentage …
A few / Only a few / A minority …
A small number / percentage of …

VOCABULARY DEVELOPMENT Word formation (1)

1 **Read STUDY SKILL** What other words can be formed from these words by adding the suffixes *-ize* or *-ation*? Use a dictionary to help.

1 Western
2 international
3 standard
4 liberal
5 modern
6 industrial
7 formal

2 Write the parts of speech in the table. Match the suffixes in the box with the words in the table. You may need to make changes to the words. Finally, write the parts of speech of the words that you form.

-ment	-ism	-less	-ist	-ness	~~-able~~

word	part of speech	word + suffix	part of speech
count	verb	countable	adjective
neurology			
plagiarize			
serious			
power			
treat			

3 Add these words to the table below. Make changes as necessary. Use a dictionary to help you. Some words can go into more than one column.

calm	hero	contain	aim	help	arrange	enjoy	improve
hard	tour	happy	change	equip	social	clean	manner

-able	-ist	-ism	-ness	-less	-ment

4 In small groups, discuss the following questions.

1 Are standardized tests a good measure of intelligence?
2 How do you define happiness?
3 How can universities stop plagiarism?

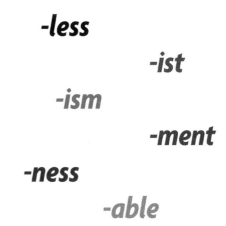

-less

-ist

-ism

-ment

-ness

-able

REVIEW

1 5.10 Listen to the discussion and match the speakers with their opinions.

1 May	A The globalization of culture is caused by people travelling.
2 Alberto	B Companies' economic interests are also a cause.
3 Rita	C Technology is the largest factor.

2 5.11 Listen to the speaker and complete the fact box.

Company: IKEA

Founded: _____

First store (in Sweden): _____

First international store: _____

Currently: _____

3 Rewrite the open questions below as closed questions. Use multiple choice, Yes / No and rating questions.

1 What kinds of films do you like?
2 What do you usually have for breakfast?
3 Which countries' cultures are you interested in?
4 Which websites do you regularly use?
5 What international foods do you enjoy?

4 Use the questions you wrote in exercise 3 to interview your partner. Make sure you:

• introduce yourself and explain the purpose of the interview.
• ask your questions and clarify the questions if necessary.
• make a note of the answers.

5 In pairs, explain the graphs.

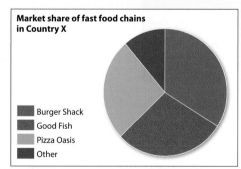

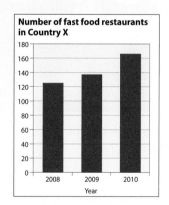

6 Choose suffixes from the box to complete the words in the sentences below.

-ness	-ist	-less	-ize	-ment

1 The university decided to standard_____ all the examinations to get a better idea of the students' level.
2 The people on the beach felt help_____ as the boat was overturned by the huge waves.
3 Sven was a heart special_____ at a large hospital in Geneva. His work on the heart won him many awards.
4 Encourage_____ by teachers can motivate students to do better.
5 The hard_____ of the metal can be increased by adding carbon to the solution.

6 History and heritage

LISTENING SKILLS Establishing criteria • Critical thinking (6) Detecting points of view and assumptions
RESEARCH Using an organization's or a company's website
SPEAKING SKILLS Summarizing data from a table • Presentations (5) The conclusion
VOCABULARY DEVELOPMENT Prefixes

LISTENING What is 'World Heritage'?

1 Read the definition of 'heritage'. What do you think 'World Heritage' means? Discuss with a partner.

2 Look at these photos. These places have all been declared UNESCO World Heritage Sites. Try to match the pictures with the names.

> **heritage** /ˈherɪtɪdʒ/ **noun** [C, usually sing.] the traditions, qualities and culture of a country that have existed for a long time and that have great importance for the country

1 Mountain railways of India ☐
2 Hiroshima Peace Memorial, Japan ☐
3 Dorset and East Devon Coast, UK ☐
4 Abu Simbel Temples, Egypt ☐

3 **Read STUDY SKILL** Work in groups and discuss the sites in the photos. Why do you think these places have been chosen as World Heritage Sites? What are the criteria that are used?

> **STUDY SKILL** Establishing criteria
>
> Criteria are the standards by which something is measured in order to make a selection. For example:
> *This should be a World Heritage site because there is no other example of this type of building in the world.*

4 Imagine you have to decide which buildings in your city / country you should conserve. What criteria would the buildings need to meet? Add four criteria to the list below. Check your list with a partner. Then think about which buildings in your city / country meet your criteria.

in good physical condition _____ _____

_____ _____

5 You are going to listen to a radio interview. Read the notes from the radio guide and answer these questions.

1 Who is being interviewed?
2 Where does he work?
3 What topics will they discuss?

6 Imagine you are interviewing Dr Olearski. What questions would you like to ask him? Make a list of six questions, including information and opinion questions. Compare your list with a partner.

WORLD REPORT:

In today's edition of World Report we are looking at the question of heritage. In our rapidly developing world much of the world's heritage, whether it is an ancient fort, an unspoilt forest, or a fine example of modern architecture, is being destroyed. How does UNESCO decide which of the world's best cultural or natural sites should be protected? And what does it mean to be selected as a World Heritage site? Dr Tomas Olearski from the UNESCO World Heritage Programme answers these and other questions.

7 6.1 Listen to the interview.

1 What kind of questions does the interviewer ask: mainly opinion, mainly factual/information or an equal balance?
2 How many of your questions were answered? Check the answers with your partner.

8 6.2 Listen to the first part of the interview again. Correct the information in the first part of this World Heritage Programme fact sheet, 'History'.

UNESCO World Heritage Programme: Fact Sheet

History

Initial idea came in 1972

Initial project: to move the Pyramids in Egypt because of rising level of the Nile

More than $8 million collected from UN members

The convention was ratified in 1987

Goal: to help build heritage sites and keep them for future generations

Convention ratified by 87 countries

---

9 6.3 Listen to the second part of the interview and complete the rest of the fact sheet: 'World Heritage Programme today' and 'How are sites selected?' Check your answers with a partner.

World Heritage Programme today

Number of sites worldwide: ^{1}_____
– cultural sites: ^{2}_____
– natural sites: ^{3}_____
– mixed: ^{4}_____
Number of countries with sites: ^{5}_____
Example of cultural sites: ^{6}_____
Example of natural sites: ^{7}_____
Example of a mixed site: ^{8}_____

How are sites selected?

Number of criteria to select sites: ^{9}_____
Procedure for getting a site recognized:

1 A country draws up a list of possible
   sites = ^{10}_____ list
2 The country adds a site from the list
   to a ^{11}_____ file
3 File is passed to ^{12}_____
4 The Committee meets and makes a decision

Conserving a historical site

1 Look at the photos of Bahla Fort in Oman. Discuss the following questions in small groups.

1 Which of these building materials were probably used in the fort's restoration?

stone	wood	concrete	glass	steel	brick	mud	marble

2 Why do you think this work was carried out on the fort?
3 Is the renovation of historical sites always a good thing? What possible drawbacks are there?

2 🎧 6.4 Listen to a speaker introducing the archaeologist Professor Rosie Sanders. What vocabulary do you expect to hear in the rest of the talk? Make a list of six words.

3 🎧 6.5 Listen to Professor Rosie Sanders's talk. The headings below refer to the slides that accompany the talk. Number them in the correct order, 1–5. Check your answers with a partner.

___ Bahla market		___ Bahla – the oasis town
___ The oasis from the top of Bahla		___ Bahla Fort viewed from the market
___ The fort under renovation		

4 🎧 6.5 Listen again and decide if the following are True (T) or False (F). Correct the false statements.

1 Wheat, barley, cotton, sugar cane and dates are the main agricultural crops in Bahla. ___
2 Bahla is an oasis containing a number of villages. ___
3 Bahla produces its own pottery. ___
4 The fort is the oldest in Oman but not the largest. ___
5 The fort was built by a powerful tribe in the region about 600 years ago. ___
6 The fort was in a very bad state but not in danger when it became a UNESCO World Heritage Site. ___
7 UNESCO has spent more than $9 million on restoring the site. ___
8 The fort is still an endangered building. ___
9 Concrete was used in rebuilding the fort. ___
10 Being a World Heritage Site means that the fort has received a lot of publicity. ___

5 Check your answers with a partner.

6 **Read STUDY SKILL** 🎧 6.5 Listen again. Discuss the following questions in pairs.

1 What is Professor Sanders's view of restoring this ancient fort? Tick (✓) more than one option.

Restoration …

☐ has spoilt the character of the building.
☐ is improving the building.
☐ has been a long and expensive procedure.
☐ will attract tourism.

2 What assumptions are there (if any)?

7 Discuss your answers in small groups. Do you agree or disagree with the speaker's views about restoration? Is it always a good thing? Use examples of other renovated buildings that you know.

8 What assumptions may lie behind the following? Discuss with a partner.

1 A talk on how to form a study group while at university.
2 A lecture on avoiding plagiarism when writing essays.
3 A presentation on how students can keep fit while at university.
4 A radio discussion on how to introduce the Internet into schools.
5 An interview with a charity on sending aid to developing countries.

> **STUDY SKILL**
> **Critical thinking (6) Detecting points of view and assumptions**
>
> It is important to be aware of the presenter's point of view.
> - What are his or her views on the topic?
> - What arguments are used to support the views?
>
> We should also be aware of any 'hidden' views or assumptions. These are not clearly stated opinions but they underlie what the speaker or writer says. Here are some examples:
> - A lecture about how to increase tourism in a developing country.
>   Assumption: Tourism is beneficial to such countries.
> - A radio programme about controlling population.
>   Assumption: The world is overpopulated.

RESEARCH Using the Internet

1 **Read STUDY SKILL** Find out about UNESCO World Heritage. Go to the World Heritage website, <http://whc. unesco.org>, if you can. Find answers to these questions:

1 How many criteria are there?
2 How many are cultural criteria? How many are natural criteria?
3 Is it possible for a site to have both cultural and natural criteria?
4 Give one example of a cultural criterion and one of a natural criterion.

Cultural: _____

Natural: _____

2 Work in groups of four. Each member of the group should choose one of the World Heritage Sites from page 44.

1 Find out about the site. How does the site meet the criteria? Make notes.
2 Describe the site to the group in your own words, and explain how the site meets the criteria.

3 Choose a World Heritage site from your country or a country you know well.

1 Find out about the site (the location, a physical description, its history, etc.) and why it has been chosen (criteria). Look also at what changes have been made or are planned for the future.
2 Make notes on the site and record the references (websites, books, articles) you use.

> **STUDY SKILL**
> **Using an organization's or a company's website**
>
> Most organizations such as unesco World Heritage or companies such as Nike have their own websites. These can be a useful source of information about:
> - the aims of the organization.
> - the range of products or services.
> - its history.
> - its organizational structure.
>
> However, it is important to remember that these websites aim to present the organization or company in its best light. They are not objective and should be used alongside more objective sources of information.

SPEAKING Presenting data

1 Look at the table. What does it show? What main points do you notice from the information? Discuss your ideas with a partner.

World Heritage Sites				
zone	natural	cultural	mixed	total
Africa	33	42	3	78
Arab States	4	60	1	65
Asia-Pacific	48	129	9	186
Europe, United States & Canada	56	375	9	440
Latin America & Caribbean	35	83	3	121
Total	**176**	**689**	**25**	**890**

2 **Read STUDY SKILL** ⊚ 6.6 Listen to two extracts from talks, A and B. The speakers describe the data in the table. Which talk is the best? Why? Why is the other not a good example?

3 ⊚ 6.6 Listen to the talks again. Make a list of the main differences between the two talks. Discuss your list with a partner.

4 Work in groups of three. Each member of the group should choose one of the tables below. Prepare a short talk for your partners summarizing the main points from the table you have chosen.

Number of tourists 2009–2011 (millions)			
Country	2009	2010	2011
Appolonia	1.35	1.32	1.36
Banderu	2.05	2.07	1.68
Canderland	0.85	1.49	2.13

University of Appolonia: Male and female student enrolment (%) by faculty – 2011						
	Urban Planning	Tourism	Science	Applied IT	Mechanical Engineering	Arts and Humanities
Male students	41.67	27.34	59.05	54.23	62.32	23.15
Female students	58.33	72.66	40.95	45.77	37.68	76.85

Visitors to main tourist sites in Canderland (2011)		
tourist site	number of visitors	average age of visitor
Royal Palace	578,539	59.7
Historical Museum	403,450	54.9
Zoo	445,085	29.3
National Art Gallery	698,332	31.4
Science Museum	287,691	40.7

STUDY SKILL
Summarizing data from a table

Tables usually contain a lot of detailed information. When we describe data in a table, it is important to pick out just the main points. Focus on:
- the title.
- a general description of the table.
- the high and low figures.
- any surprising or unexpected figures.

It is not necessary to read out every figure in the table.

Concluding your presentation

1 Discuss the questions in small groups.

1 What is the main aim of the conclusion of a talk or presentation?
2 How is it different from the introduction?

2 [Read STUDY SKILL] Look again at this quotation from Unit 2:

> **'Tell them what you are going to tell them. Tell them.**
> **Then tell them what you've told them.'**

Discuss the quotation in pairs. What do you think the conclusion of a talk should include?

3 🎧 **6.7** Listen to three speakers, A, B and C. They are concluding a talk they have given on a World Heritage Site. Decide which conclusion is the best. Why are the other two conclusions not good examples?

4 Prepare a five-minute presentation on the site that you researched on page 47. Complete the table to help you structure your presentation and include two or three slides or other visuals. Use expressions from the Language Bank.

PRESENTATION PLAN	your notes / key words
Introduction – site	
Location – country / region / city?	
Physical description – What is it like?	
History of the site – How old is it?	
When was the site selected by World Heritage?	
Why was it was chosen? Criteria?	
What changes have been made? Renovations?	
Conclusion – Recommendations? What will happen to the site in the future?	

LANGUAGE BANK The language of conclusions

Summarizing:
To sum up … / To summarize …
Today, I've talked about / discussed …
My aim in this presentation was to …

Concluding:
To conclude … / In conclusion …
I'd like to conclude by saying …

Recommending:
I (strongly) recommend that …
One of my recommendations is that …

Questions:
If there are any questions, I'd be happy to …
Does anyone have a question?

---

5 Give your presentation to the class. Make sure you give a strong conclusion.

VOCABULARY DEVELOPMENT Word formation (2)

1 **Read STUDY SKILL** Match the words in bold with the meanings. Use the prefixes to help.

give out in a different way	below the earth
see before	not easy to believe
cannot be maintained	not meet the requirements
think again about something	form an opinion before seeing the evidence

1 The building was **substandard** and had to be pulled down. _____

2 It is possible to **preview** a document before printing it. _____

3 Agriculture was **unsustainable** in that arid climate. _____

4 The professor said he would **reconsider** the student's grade. _____

5 We shouldn't **prejudge** the issue. The man may be completely innocent of this crime. _____

6 The earthquake was caused by a **subterranean** movement of tectonic plates. _____

7 The manager said he would **redistribute** the tasks after some staff complained of too much work. _____

8 The students thought the lecturer's argument on the world food crisis was **unconvincing**. _____

2 Look at the words and phrases in the box. They include a number of different prefixes. Try to work out the meanings of the words or phrases from the context. Use a dictionary if necessary. Then complete the sentences.

illogical	intranet	postgraduate	disassembled
undervalued	overestimated	mismanaged	extracurricular

1 The university offered students many _____ activities, such as mountain climbing, chess, badminton and meditation.

2 Fortunately, they had _____ the cost of the project and more than $5.5 million remained when they had finished.

3 As a _____ student studying for his doctorate, Ahmed was able to spend most of his time at home or in the library.

4 Before the college installed the _____ , staff had to rely mainly on the telephone or memos to communicate with their colleagues.

5 Because of the flood the building was _____ and moved to another location, where it was put back together again.

6 The instruction seemed _____ but Sarah decided to do what she was told.

7 The project was _____ right from the beginning. As a result, a lot of time and money was wasted.

8 Steve felt _____ as an employee. He had worked for the company for four years and had never had a pay rise.

Prefixes, such as *re-*, *pre-*, *un-*, and *sub-*, are placed at the beginning of words. For example:

predate, unattractive, subway

Prefixes can help us to understand new words. For example, the prefix *re-* usually carries the idea of 'again'.

rewrite, reconstruct, rebuild.

re-

pre-

il-

mis-

sub-

REVIEW

1 🔊 6.8 Listen to an interview and answer the questions.

1 What kind of help does the preservation committee provide?
2 What criteria are used by the committee?

2 🔊 6.8 Listen again. Write the questions that the interviewer asks:

1 to get factual information.
2 to obtain clarification.
3 to get opinions.
4 to develop the discussion.

3 Read the statements. What underlying assumptions are there? Discuss in pairs.

1 This must be an excellent laptop. It cost more than $1,000.
2 I wouldn't buy a Zippo car. My brother's car broke down on the motorway last week and it was only two years old.
3 Shares in mining companies are at an all-time low. It is probably a good time to buy.
4 There is good news for air passengers today. The airport is to double in size.
5 There is a disappointing weather forecast for Spain today – cloudy with rain in most parts.

A stonemason doing restoration work

4 Working in pairs, summarize the information on the table.

historic buildings in Cambford					
site	year built	height	visitors per year	funding received per year	maintenance costs per year
Old Town Hall	1780	25 metres	3,000	£9,000	£10,000
Mill House	1689	60 metres	5,000	£8,000	£7,000
The Alston Building	1926	65 metres	300	£7,000	£25,000

5 Tick (✓) the sentences which would probably appear in the conclusion of a presentation.

1 ☐ I'd strongly recommend that you look further at some of the websites listed in the handout.
2 ☐ Today I'm going to talk about the UNESCO-listed town centre of Lviv.
3 ☐ If there are any questions, I'd be happy to answer them now.
4 ☐ I'd like to conclude by saying that this is only the beginning of our work in these regions.
5 ☐ Let me explain further: without adequate funding, these projects can not be started.
6 ☐ Today, I've discussed several ways in which preservation sites benefit society.

7 Developments in architecture

LISTENING SKILLS Making inferences • Recognizing the plan of a talk • Mind mapping
SPEAKING SKILLS Critical thinking (7) Supporting a point of view • Preparing visuals
VOCABULARY DEVELOPMENT Learning subject-specific vocabulary

LISTENING Airports around the world

1 Look at the photos of the airports and answer the questions below in pairs.

1 What do you notice about the structures? What building materials do you think they are made of?
2 What words would you use to describe the airport buildings? Make a list of ten words.
3 What airports have you been to? What types of buildings did you notice there? What facilities were there for passengers?
4 What do you think are the problems in constructing airports? What do the architects need to consider?

2 🎧 7.1 Listen to this description of modern airports and airport terminals and answer the questions.

1 What facility do all airports have in common?
2 What buildings do airports usually have?
3 What is the main function of a terminal?

3 🎧 7.2 Listen to the podcast 'Airports around the world' and answer the questions.

1 Which airport is the world's largest?
2 Which was voted the world's best?
3 Which new terminal buildings are described at each airport?

4 🎧 7.2 Listen to the podcast again. Complete the table with information about each airport.

Airports of the world	1	2	3
Name			
City			
Date completed			
Architects			
Size of terminal building (m²)			
Special design features			

Changi Airport, Singapore

Beijing Capital International Airport

Barajas, Madrid

5 [Read STUDY SKILL] What inferences can you make from the following information? Discuss your answers with a partner.

1 Large buildings such as airport terminals need strong materials to support them. Steel is used in the construction of many such buildings.

2 A large new terminal, Terminal 3, was opened last year. Already another even larger terminal is being planned.

3 Airport terminals are places where passengers buy tickets, transfer their luggage and then board their planes. But they also contain restaurants, shops and relaxation areas for passengers.

6 7.3 Listen carefully to these extracts from the podcast about the Beijing International Airport. What conclusions can you infer from the information? Tick (✓) one option for each extract.

1

☐ Beijing Capital International Airport isn't the biggest airport in the world.

☐ Other, larger airports may be built in the future.

☐ They are planning to expand the airport further.

2

☐ The airport was built as part of the preparation for the Beijing Olympics.

☐ The Olympic Games were held in Beijing in 2008.

☐ The airport would have been built with or without the Olympics.

3

☐ Dragons are an important part of Chinese culture.

☐ The airport is shaped like a dragon.

☐ Red and golden yellow are traditional Chinese colours.

---

7 Discuss the questions below in groups.
1 Each of the three airports or terminal buildings has something special which makes it unique. What is it?
2 Why do you think the architects did this? What were their motives?
3 Why do countries like to have modern international airports?

8 Imagine you were designing an airport for your country or city. Work in small groups and discuss the following points:
1 What kind of airport would you design?
2 What materials would you use?
3 What shape would the airport be?
4 How would you make it special or unique?

STUDY SKILL Making inferences

In talks and presentations, listeners are often presented with information about a topic but are not given clear conclusions. You are left to make inferences or draw your own conclusions, e.g.:

■ *The new terminal building is very sustainable in its design. For example, it makes great use of natural light.*

From this description of the building, you can probably make the following inference:

■ *A lot of glass was used in the construction of the building.*

Green skyscrapers

Pearl River Tower, China

Bank of America Tower, New York

1 Look at the photos of the two skyscrapers with a partner.

1 Describe the two buildings. Try to give a definition of a skyscraper.
2 Why do you think people want to build such tall buildings?
3 What do you think a 'green' skyscraper is? In what ways will it be different from a normal building? Make a list of points.

2 **Read STUDY SKILL** 7.4 Look at the plans of a talk on green skyscrapers. Listen to the introduction to the lecture. Which of the following, A, B or C, represents the outline of the talk?

A

Examples of two green skyscrapers

Some of the features of these green buildings

Definition of green architecture

B

Some of the features of these green buildings

Definition of green architecture

Examples of two green skyscrapers

C

Definition of green architecture

Examples of two green skyscrapers

Some of the features of these green buildings

STUDY SKILL
Recognizing the plan of a talk

It is important to recognize a presenter's plan. This helps listening and note-taking throughout the talk. Note phrases such as:

- *First I want to talk about ...*
- *The first section will concern ...*
- *Then I'll move onto the question of ...*
- *After that I want to explore ...*
- *Finally, I'd like to discuss ...*
- *I'll conclude by examining ...*

3 **Read STUDY SKILL** 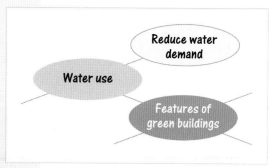 7.5 Now listen to the second part of the talk.

1 Give two features of a green building.
2 Copy and complete the mind map on the right with the main features of green buildings and other important points.
3 Compare your mind map with a partner. Is any information missing?

STUDY SKILL Mind mapping

Mind maps start with an idea or topic in the centre of the page and work outwards. This type of note-taking is more flexible. It helps you to make connections between points. For example:

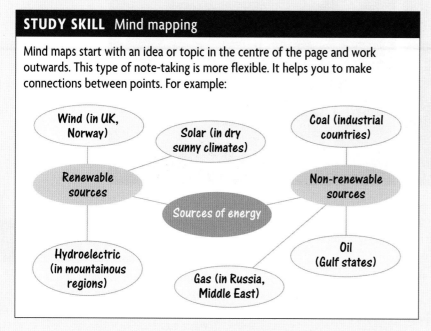

---

4 Use your notes from exercise 3 to answer the questions about the talk.

1 How can water use be reduced in a building? Give an example.
2 What alternative sources of energy can a building use?
3 How can builders reduce the amount of energy that is needed?
4 What does 'sustainable' mean?
5 Give an example of a sustainable building material.
6 How can a building's waste be reduced?

5 7.6 Listen to the rest of the talk. Make a mind map about each building.

Pearl River Tower   Bank of America Tower

6 Use your notes from exercise 5 to decide if these statements are True (T) or False (F). Correct the false statements.

1 The Pearl River Tower is located in Beijing. ___
2 The tower has 55 storeys. ___
3 The tower is exactly 309 metres high. ___
4 The wind provides some of its power. ___
5 Radiant cooling is cooling by the use of water pipes in the walls of the building. ___
6 The Bank of America Tower is 78 metres high. ___
7 It is situated in the centre of New York. ___
8 Construction of the tower was completed in 2010. ___
9 The building will use 70% less energy than ordinary buildings. ___
10 The walls are glass, so most of the lighting is natural lighting. ___

7 Work in pairs. Use your notes to give an oral description of one of the two buildings.

SPEAKING Supporting your argument

1 Look at the photos of Hong Kong and Mumbai and discuss them with a partner. What do you notice about the two cities? Which city do you think has the highest density of population? Why?

Hong Kong

Mumbai

2 | Read STUDY SKILL | 7.7 Listen to the speaker introducing a debate on skyscrapers and answer the following questions.

    1 What is the speaker's point of view about skyscrapers?

    2 In what ways does she support her view?

3 Work in groups and prepare to discuss the following issue:

'Skyscrapers are not beneficial to cities.'

    1 Divide into two teams – those in favour of the statement and those against.

    2 Prepare arguments to support your point of view. Each team should have one speaker to present the case and one or two speakers to add support.

4 7.8 Listen to an extract from a discussion.

    1 What is the topic of the discussion?

    2 What are the speakers' views on the topic? Who is in favour and who is against?

    3 Which three points are raised during the discussion?

    4 How do the speakers agree and disagree? Make a note of phrases they use.

5 Using the expressions in the Language Bank, discuss whether skyscrapers are beneficial to cities.

STUDY SKILL Critical thinking (7)
Supporting a point of view

To present a strong argument it is important to be able to support your views. You can do this in a number of ways, e.g.:

- giving examples.
- presenting evidence (facts and figures).
- quoting the conclusions of studies or reports.
- recognizing the opposing view (but saying why this view is wrong).

At the same time you should avoid:

- emotive language.
- personal anecdotes (stories about what happened to you).
- exaggerating or simplifying the opposing view.

LANGUAGE BANK Agreeing and disagreeing

Opinions	Agreeing	Disagreeing
I think / I (firmly) believe …	*I (completely) agree with …*	*I (completely) disagree / I don't agree with … at all.*
It seems to me …	*You are (absolutely) right …*	*I don't think that's completely true.*
I take the view that …	*I'm in complete agreement (with …)*	*I'm afraid I can't agree …*
I've always believed …	*That's a very good point …*	*I can't accept that (I'm afraid) …*
As far as I'm concerned …		*I see / take your point but …*
It's clear to me …		*I understand what you are saying, but nevertheless …*

---

6 Review your discussion with the rest of the class.

    1 What were the main arguments (for and against)?

    2 How did the speakers support their views?

    3 Who had the strongest arguments?

Describing visuals

1 **Read STUDY SKILL** Look at the visuals below. Work with a partner and describe the visuals. In what way are they suitable or not suitable for a presentation on the World Trade Centre in Bahrain?

The two towers are linked via three skybridges each holding a 225 KW wind turbine totalling 675 KW of wind power production. Each of these turbines measure 29 m (95 ft) in diameter, and is aligned north, which is the direction from which wind from the Gulf blows in. The sail-shaped buildings on either side are designed to funnel wind through the gap to provide accelerated wind passing through the turbines.

A

**towers 240m,
linked by 3 skybridges**

• hold 225KW wind turbine
turbines are 29m in diameter
face north **for prevailing wind**

B

towers:
– 240 m high
– linked by three skybridges
– each hold 225 KW wind turbine

turbines:
– measure 29m in diameter
– face north

C

Wind turbine

D

World Trade Centre, Bahrain

E

F

STUDY SKILL Preparing visuals

Visuals to accompany a presentation are usually in the form of:

■ pictures   ■ graphics   ■ notes (in bullet form)

Depending on the technology available, speakers can use PowerPoint slides, overhead transparencies or posters. Here are a few rules for good visuals:

■ Make sure the information can be clearly seen by the audience.
■ Use the same format and font (letter style / size) throughout.
■ Do not put too much information on one visual.
■ Display each graphic separately.
■ Use bullet points to make the information easier to see.

The best slides often have the least information.

2 7.9 Listen to a short presentation about the World Trade Centre in Bahrain. Choose three of the visuals from exercise 1 to accompany the talk. Put them in the correct order.

3 Choose a building that you know and research information about it. Find information on some or all of the following:

location   history   date of completion   height   capacity   building materials
any renovations or rebuilding   architects   green features

4 Prepare a short, five-minute talk on the building. Include an introduction, a main body, and a conclusion in your plan. Prepare two or three visuals to illustrate the talk.

5 Working in groups of four, give your presentations. Take notes.

VOCABULARY DEVELOPMENT Subject-specific vocabulary

1 **Read STUDY SKILL** Read the short texts below about architecture. Are the underlined words subject-specific or general vocabulary?

> 1 A <u>dormer</u> is a structural element of a building that protrudes from a sloping surface. Dormers are used, either in original construction or as later additions, to create usable space in the <u>roof</u> of a building by adding headroom and windows.
>
> 2 A <u>geodesic dome</u> is a sphere-like <u>structure</u> composed of a complex network of triangles. The triangles create a self-bracing framework that gives <u>structural</u> strength while using a minimum of material.
>
> 3 A series of columns or arches in front of a building is known as a <u>portico</u>. It forms a covered walkway that protects people from the sun or rain.
>
> 4 <u>Tensile</u> architecture refers to <u>structures</u> formed mostly of components acting in <u>tension</u>, rather than <u>compression</u>. It might include tents, suspension bridges and suspended roofs, where weight can determine the form of the structure and its <u>stability</u>.

A geodesic dome

STUDY SKILL Learning subject-specific vocabulary

You will need to learn vocabulary that is specific to your subject.

It is helpful to arrange vocabulary into a number of sub-divisions within the subject area, for example:

Civil Engineering: statics, soil mechanics, fluid mechanics, structural engineering, engineering materials.

Remember too that some common words can have very specific meanings in some subject areas, for example:

- *matter, charge* engineering
- *cost, elasticity* economics
- *plate, fault* geology

2 Study the subject-specific words and phrases below. Categorize them according to subject area. You can use a subject-specific dictionary to help you.

monetarism	mucous	buttress	hedge funds	cholesterol	lattice
constructivism	tariff	pancreas	tangible assets	rafter	tumour

Medicine	Architecture	Economics

3 Find ten words that are related to your subject and add them to your vocabulary records. Make a note of the following:

- part of speech (noun, verb, adjective, etc.)
- pronunciation
- meaning or meanings
- different forms of the word (e.g. *architect, architecture, architectural*)
- collocations (*contemporary architecture, architectural design*)
- examples of use in a sentence
- translation

REVIEW

Fallingwater house by Frank Lloyd Wright

1 🔊 **7.10** Listen to the talk about organic architecture. Draw a mind map. Include information about the style, architects and buildings.

Organic architecture

2 🔊 **7.10** Listen again and tick (✓) the summary sentences which are inferences.
- ☐ Organic architecture is not the same as green architecture.
- ☐ Most modern architecture uses flat shapes and straight lines.
- ☐ Antoni Gaudí wanted people to feel like they were entering a cave when they entered Casa Milà.
- ☐ Fallingwater was designed by Frank Lloyd Wright.
- ☐ Fallingwater does not look out of place.

3 In pairs, discuss the topic. One person should be for and the other against. Use the ideas in the table as well as your own ideas.

modern buildings in historic city centres	
for:	**against:**
Cities need more housing and offices.	Modern buildings can change the historic look or character of the city centre.
Modern buildings can be more environmentally-friendly than older buildings.	City centres are already too crowded.
Modern buildings can be attractive.	Modern buildings should be built outside the centre, where there is more space.

4 Match the subject-specific vocabulary with the subjects. Use a dictionary if necessary.

1 ☐ microprocessors		a	environmental science
2 ☐ subsidiaries		b	architecture
3 ☐ neurological		c	medicine
4 ☐ lintel		d	IT
5 ☐ ecosystem		e	economics

5 Complete the sentences with the subject-specific vocabulary from exercise 4.
1 To raise capital, the company sold off several of its _____ .
2 The effects of the refinery on the region's fragile _____ were noticeable immediately.
3 The stone _____ over the main entryway is carved to resemble the front of a boat.
4 After several days of dizziness, he was sent to a specialist centre for _____ examinations.
5 Commercial desktops now have several times their predecessors' performance capabilities due to multi-core _____ .

8 The sports industry

LISTENING SKILLS Recognizing the structure of an interview • Reviewing and organizing notes
RESEARCH Using keywords in research
SPEAKING SKILLS Successful interviews • Presentations (6) Logical organization • Establishing rapport
VOCABULARY DEVELOPMENT Word families

LISTENING Sports sponsorship

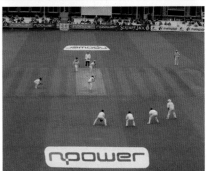

1 Look at the photos. Identify the logos and the sports.

2 Complete the short text about sports sponsorship using the words in the box.

> return   sponsorship   funds   which   organization   business

> **Sports sponsorship** is a ¹_____ relationship between a provider of
> ²_____, resources or services and an individual, event or
> ³_____ involved in sport, ⁴_____ offers in return rights and
> association that may be used for commercial advantage in ⁵_____ for
> the ⁶_____ investment.

3 Discuss the questions with a partner.
   1 Which sports have the most sponsorship? Why is this?
   2 What examples of sponsorship can you think of in sport? Try to make a
      classification of different types, for example: sponsorship of competitions.
   3 Is sponsorship a good thing or a bad thing for sport?

4 🔊 8.1 Listen to the introduction to a radio programme 'Business Now' on
      the subject of sports sponsorship. Make notes while you listen. Use them to
      answer these questions.
   1 When and where did sponsorship start?
   2 How did FIFA earn $1.6 billion and when?
   3 Which individuals or organizations does the presenter mention that are
      affected by sponsorship?

5 Read STUDY SKILL 🔘 8.2 Listen to the rest of the programme. It contains an interview with a sports journalist, Leo Desa. As you listen, number the topics he mentions in the correct order.

___ sports which attract sponsorship
___ disadvantages of sponsorship
___ the future of sports sponsorship
___ definition of sports sponsorship
___ advantages of sponsorship
___ what companies get out of sponsorship

STUDY SKILL Recognizing the structure of an interview

Recognizing the sequence of topics will help you to follow the interview when listening. Listen for signals from the interviewer, e.g.

I'd like to start by asking you ...
Now let's turn to the question of ...
I'd like to move on to ...
Now what do you think about ...?

---

6 🔘 8.2 Listen to the interview again. Are the sentences True (T) or False (F)? Correct the false statements.

1 Individuals, teams and events can all be sponsored. ___
2 Sponsorship is a kind of charity. ___
3 Tennis, baseball and football attract the most sponsorship internationally. ___
4 Sponsorship has meant that standards in sport have fallen. ___
5 All sports get equal attention from sponsors. ___
6 Sometimes sponsors want to change the rules in a sport. ___
7 Leo Desa thinks that sponsorship has been good for sport. ___

7 🔘 8.3 Listen to the last part of the interview again. Make a list of the advantages and disadvantages of sponsorship that are mentioned.

8 Discuss your lists with the rest of the class. What are your opinions about sports sponsorship?

The science of sport

1 Look at the photos and answer the questions.
1 Why do you think they are successful in their sports? Make a list of the factors involved in an excellent sporting performance.
2 In what ways do you think science can help successful sportsmen and women?

2 Think about something that you were successful in: a sport, a pastime, a driving test, an examination, a competition, etc. How did you prepare? How did you become successful? Discuss in small groups.

3 🔘 8.4 Listen to the introduction to the talk on 'Sport and Science' and take notes. Use your notes to answer these questions.
1 What is the aim of the talk?
2 Which five factors in achieving sporting success does the speaker mention?

Lionel Messi

Caroline Wozniacki

Oscar Pastorius

4 🎧 8.5 Listen to the main body of the talk and take notes on the five factors. Use a mind map or linear notes.

5 🎧 8.6 Listen to the conclusion of the talk and take notes.

6 Use your notes from exercises 4 and 5 to answer these questions. Work with a partner and compare your ideas.

1 What is sports physiology?
2 What are the three classes of food?
3 Which is most important as fuel for athletes?
4 What were tennis racquets made of in the past?
5 What are they made of now?
6 What is performance analysis?
7 Give examples of two psychological factors that can affect sport.
8 Summarize the conclusion.

Gold medal winners

7 **Read STUDY SKILL** Look at the notes below with a partner. They describe three of the factors mentioned in the lecture.

1 What is wrong with the notes? How could they be improved?
2 Rewrite the notes in a more organized way, using a mind map or linear notes.

sports physiology   we can help athletes
running, jumping
functioning of body
we learn how the body works
food and drink   carbohydrates   proteins
nutrition
three classes   fats   sports equipment
tennis racquet
sports technology   football boots

STUDY SKILL Reviewing and organizing notes

After a lecture it is a good idea to review your notes while the topic is still fresh in your mind. To improve your notes you can:

■ read through and complete any missing information (check with another student).
■ highlight important information (use colour or underlining).
■ show relationships between information (e.g. use arrows and circles).
■ add comments at the sides of the notes.
■ if necessary, rewrite the notes completely in a more organized way.

---

8 Follow the steps to review your notes from exercises 3, 4, and 5.

1 Review your notes and add any missing information.
2 Organize the notes by showing important pieces of information and the relationships between them.
3 Rewrite the notes if you think this is necessary, or if it will help you to remember the content of the lecture.

RESEARCH Keywords

1 **Read STUDY SKILL** Read the list of presentation titles below. What sources would you use to find the necessary information? What are the keywords in each title? Underline them.

> 1 The effects of global warming on the ice caps of the polar regions.
> 2 The costs of nuclear power compared to other sources of renewable energy.
> 3 The relationship between academic performance and physical fitness amongst school children.
> 4 The role of continental drift in the formation of the Himalayan mountain range.

STUDY SKILL Using keywords in research

To get information on a specific topic you can use a variety of sources, including a library database and the Internet. Use keywords to help you find the specific information you need. For example, to research the following essay:

'Discuss the effect of sports nutrition on the performance of athletes. Explain the key role of protein.'

The keywords you need are:
sports, nutrition, athletes, protein

Note that in an Internet search, using words in speech marks, e.g. *"sports nutrition"* will produce results where these words appear together.

---

2 Work in groups of four. Each member should choose one of the presentation titles. Use the keywords to find information on the topics. Make brief notes and give a reference for the source(s) you used.

3 Explain to the rest of your group:
1 how you carried out the research (the keywords and the sources you used).
2 what information you found on the topic.

4 Choose one of the following companies and research information on how it is involved in sports sponsorship. Use keywords to help you in your search.

> Nike   Coca-Cola   Hyundai   Visa   Adidas   Cadbury's   Vodafone

Complete the table with the information you find.

Internet research	
Company	
How long involved in sponsorship	
Sports they sponsor	
Type of sponsorship	
How to get sponsored by the company	
Other	

SPEAKING Interviewing

1 Discuss the questions with a partner.

  1 Look at the photo. What kind of interview do you think this is?

  2 What do you think makes a good interviewer and a good interviewee?

2 8.7 Listen to the introductions to two interviews, A and B. Discuss with a partner which one is better. List the reasons for your choices.

3 **Read STUDY SKILL** Check the lists you made in exercise 1 and add any other points.

An interview

STUDY SKILL Successful interviews
An interviewer:
■ is well prepared.
■ has a number of clearly planned questions.
■ can ask follow-up questions.
■ is an active listener.
■ maintains a friendly and relaxed atmosphere.
An interviewee:
■ is well prepared.
■ answers the questions directly and fully.
■ does not give one-word answers.
■ can add additional information or opinions when it is relevant.

4 Look through this list of questions for an interview with a sports agent. Work in pairs and discuss which are good interview questions and which are not. Give reasons for your answers.

  1 Have you represented many well-known athletes?

  2 Could you tell us which well-known athletes you've represented?

  3 Could you tell us what kind of things sports agents do for their clients?

  4 What do you think is the role of sports agents?

  5 Do you negotiate contracts for sponsorships with big companies?

  6 Could you explain what you mean by that?

  7 Do you think sports agents are necessary for professional athletes?

  8 Why are sports agents important for professional athletes?

5 Work in pairs. Use the role cards to prepare and conduct interviews about sports sponsorship.

A	B
Interviewer	Company representative
Decide what topics to cover.	Review information on the company you researched.
Plan interview.	Be prepared to answer questions.
Write suitable questions.	

Logical organization

1 Look at the tennis racquets in the photos. Discuss the questions with a partner.

1 Which of the racquets is more modern?
2 How have they changed in shape?
3 What other changes to the racquet do you think have taken place?
4 How do you think science has influenced the design of these racquets?

2 **Read STUDY SKILL** 🔊 8.8 Listen to this introduction to a talk on the development of tennis racquets.

1 Make a note of the four main points the lecturer is going to discuss.
2 What logical organization does the presenter use?

> ### STUDY SKILL Presentations (6) Logical organization
>
> There are many ways of organizing a presentation. For example:
> - listing factors
> - comparison (of two places, events, methods, etc.)
> - a point of view – supporting evidence
> - advantages and disadvantages
> - classifying

3 Imagine you are giving a talk on one of the following topics. How would you divide the talk? Discuss your ideas with a partner.

- How tennis racquets are made
- How to become a champion
- Why sports sponsorship is bad for sport
- Types of sponsorship

4 **Read STUDY SKILL** 🔊 8.8 Listen again. How does the speaker establish rapport with the audience? List some of the techniques he uses.

> ### LANGUAGE BANK Rapport
>
> Audience's experience:
> *Most of you probably think of … (food, cafes and art) … when you think of … (Paris) …*
> *I know some people in this room are from …*
> *As all of you probably know, …*
>
> Anecdote:
> *When I was in Paris last year, I met …*
> *I remember when … / A few years ago …*
> *An interesting thing happened to me … (on the way to the lecture)*
>
> Questions:
> *How many people … (have visited Paris)?*
> *Has anyone here ever … (asked themselves why …?)*
> *Are there any people here … (from France?)*

> ### STUDY SKILL
> ### Establishing rapport
>
> It is often useful to establish rapport with an audience. You can do this by:
> - including the audience's own experience
> - telling an anecdote
> - asking questions

5 Choose a topic from exercise 3 or one of your own choice and plan a short presentation:

- Find out information about the topic. Make a note of any sources.
- Decide which information is important and plan the talk.
- Use a logical sequence of headings for the body of the talk.
- How will you establish rapport?
- Practise your presentation to make sure it is the right length.
- Give your presentation to the class. Ask for questions at the end.

VOCABULARY DEVELOPMENT Word families

1 **Read STUDY SKILL** Look at the dictionary entries for *succeed* and *success*. Use the information to complete the table.

verb	noun	adjective	adverb

succeed 🔑 /sək'siːd/ *verb* **1** [I] ~ (in sth/doing sth) to manage to achieve what you want; to do well: *Our plan succeeded.* ◊ *A good education will help you succeed in life.* ◊ *to succeed in passing an exam* **OPP fail** ➜ noun **success 2** [I,T] to have a job or important position after sb else: *Who succeeded Kennedy as president?* ➜ noun **succession**

success 🔑 /sək'ses/ *noun* **1** [U] the fact that you have achieved what you want; doing well and becoming famous, rich, etc.: *Hard work is **the key to success**.* ◊ *Her attempts to get a job for the summer have not **met with much success** (=she hasn't managed to do it).* ◊ *What's the secret of your success?* **2** [C] the thing that you achieve; sth that becomes very popular: *He really tried to **make a success of** the business.* ◊ *The film 'Titanic' was a huge success.* **OPP failure**

STUDY SKILL Word families

It's important to learn the other members of the word family – verbs, nouns, adjectives, adverbs – that are related to the word. For example, the verb *sponsor*:

verb	noun	adjective	adverb
sponsor	sponsor sponsorship	sponsored	—
motivate	motivation motivator	motivational	motivationally

2 Use a dictionary to complete the table with members of the word families.

verb	noun	adjective	adverb
benefit			beneficially
		analytical	
—	technology		
	drama		
		relaxing, relaxed	—
	performer	performing	—

-ship
-tion
-ial
-ially

3 Complete the sentences with words from the table.

1 Tests show that exercise generally has a _____ effect on academic studies. Students tend to get slightly higher grades.
2 Hussain's _____ in the last Olympics was disappointing. He came last in the 100 metres.
3 Listening to the radio or going for long walks are ways that people can _____ when they are feeling stressed.
4 After the game, the coach and his players looked at the result _____ . What went wrong? Why did they lose? How could they do better next time?
5 The training course was very motivational. After finishing it the students' attitude to their work changed _____ .
6 Using steel instead of wood for a tennis racquet was a real _____ breakthrough. The racquet was much stronger and easier to use.

REVIEW

1 ◉ 8.9 Listen to an interview about sponsorship and put the points in the correct order. There is one extra point which is not mentioned in the interview.

☐ Risks involved in sponsorship
☐ Deciding who to sponsor
☐ Sponsoring teams
☐ Benefits of sponsorship for companies
☐ Benefits of sponsorship for athletes

2 ◉ 8.9 Listen again. Organize and complete the notes.

> sponsorship   teams   publicity
> individuals   endorse products   image   benefits
> risks   successful   good-looking   charisma   scandal

3 Rewrite the *Yes / No* interview questions below as more open *Wh-* questions. They can be both factual and opinion.

1 Do you think distance learning is a good idea?
2 Would you study a course by distance?
3 Is distance learning suitable for all people?
4 Can we study all subjects by distance?
5 Are there any disadvantages to distance learning?

4 Decide what logical organization these talks have and number the headings in a logical order. The introductions and conclusions are already in place.

1 Internet addiction
Introduction
☐ Will these solutions work?
☐ Why is it a problem?
☐ What is Internet addiction? Definition
☐ How many people are affected?
☐ Possible solutions
Conclusion

2 The development of computers
Introduction
☐ Digital computers
☐ Where do we go from here?
☐ Desktop calculators
☐ Current computers
☐ Analogue computers
Conclusion

5 Complete the sentences with words from the box.

> sponsor   motivate   succeed   commerce
> sponsorship   motivation   success   commercial
> sponsored   motivational   successful   commercialization

1 Miriam took part in a _____ 10-kilometre run last week and raised £400 for charity.
2 Some sports fans dislike the recent _____ of sport through advertising and sponsorship.
3 The training course was extremely _____ . Yuki's performance at work improved greatly after completing it.
4 _____ cannot always be quantified. For example, it is difficult to measure good public relations, a good reputation or happiness.
5 A good lecturer should be able to _____ his or her students so that they perform to their maximum potential.

LISTENING SKILLS Interpreting data in maps • Recognizing tentative language • Recognizing lecture styles
• Getting the most out of visuals
SPEAKING SKILLS Describing results in a presentation • Analyzing data critically • Presenting a survey report
VOCABULARY DEVELOPMENT Recognizing multiple meanings

LISTENING Trends in world population

1 Look at the photos and discuss the questions in small groups.

1 What do the photos show?
2 Do you think the world is becoming over-populated?
3 Why do some countries have high population growth and others low rates of growth (or negative growth)? What are the factors involved?
4 Why is it important for governments to learn about population growth in their country?

2 **Read STUDY SKILL** Look at the map and the key below in your groups. It shows the percentage of population growth in all of the countries of the world.

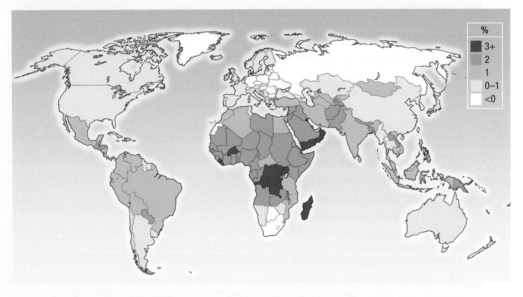

%	
	3+
	2
	1
	0–1
	<0

1 Discuss any patterns you can see in the data. Where are there high and low rates of population growth?
2 What do countries with high rates have in common?
3 What do countries with low rates have in common?
4 What exceptions are there?
5 What factors do you think may influence these differences in population growth rates?

STUDY SKILL Interpreting data in maps

When listening to a presentation it is important to understand data in maps and draw conclusions from it. We can do this by:

■ looking for patterns by country or region.

■ asking what these countries or regions have in common.

■ noting any exceptions to the pattern.

3 ⊚ **9.1** You are going to listen to a discussion on population growth rates around the world. Listen for the main ideas and decide what conclusions the participants reach on the following topics.

1 The world population and the current rate of growth.
2 The regional distribution of growth over the world.
3 The causes of the variation in growth rates.
4 Why governments need population growth statistics.
5 Future trends in world population growth.

4 ⊚ **9.1** Listen again and focus on the data. Decide if the following statements are True (T) or False (F). Correct the false statements.

1 The world population is currently around 7 billion. ___
2 It is predicted to increase to over 10.5 billion by 2050. ___
3 The present rate of increase is higher now than it was in the 1960s. ___
4 Germany and Italy have very low growth rates. ___
5 The natural growth rate includes migration. ___
6 The overall growth rate is calculated from births and deaths. ___
7 Countries such as South Korea and Japan have low birth rates. ___
8 The world's population is rising but the birth rate is falling. ___

5 Read STUDY SKILL ⊚ **9.2** Read the statements below. Listen to extracts from the discussion and notice how the speakers make these statements more tentative. Make a note of the language they use. Compare your answers with a partner.

> 1 **Yuki Masaoka:**
> Some regions have a very high growth rate – for example Sub-Saharan Africa.
>
> 2 **Yuki Masaoka:**
> People don't stay at home – people move to other countries.
>
> 3 **Dr Charles Robertson:**
> In the Middle East, in countries such as Oman and Yemen, the population growth rates are high. That is due to a high birth rate.
>
> 4 **Dr Charles Robertson:**
> There are many reasons for that. People want to have smaller families.
>
> 5 **Yuki Masaoka:**
> Another factor is that immigrants to these countries have more children.
>
> 6 **Yuki Masaoka:**
> At the moment we see two trends – the world population is rising but the birth rate throughout the world is falling as families want fewer children.
>
> 7 **Yuki Masaoka:**
> And sooner or later, if this trend in birth rates continues, the world population will fall later in the 21st century – as early as 2040.

STUDY SKILL
Recognizing tentative language

Speakers sometimes use tentative language to talk about data when they are not certain of the patterns or relationships in the data and are cautious about drawing conclusions. They use expressions such as:

- *From the data **it seems that** there is a correlation between …*
- *Population growth in Asia **tends to be** greater than population growth in …*
- ***It is likely** that this trend will continue …*
- ***In general** we can see …*

6 Discuss the following problems in groups. What possible solutions are there?

1 A country such as Italy has a very low growth rate and an ageing population.
2 A country such as Ethiopia has a very high growth rate and a young population.
3 The world's population could increase by more than 3 billion by 2050.

Is life getting better?

1 Do the people in the photos look happy? What is happiness? Can we measure it? How happy are you? Discuss your ideas with a partner.

2 Do the questionnaire and find your score. Compare with a partner.

How happy are you?

Below are a number of statements about happiness. Show how much you agree by writing the number 1–5 (5 = strongly agree, 1 = strongly disagree)

1 I am interested in other people. _____

2 I feel that life is very rewarding. _____

3 I usually wake up feeling rested. _____

4 I am optimistic about the future. _____

5 I find beauty in some things. _____

6 I feel that I am in control of my life. _____

7 I find it easy to make decisions. _____

8 I have a sense of meaning and purpose in my life. _____

9 I feel I have a great deal of energy. _____

10 I feel healthy. _____

KEY: How did you score?

Mostly 4s and 5s: You're a happy person!

Mostly 3s: You're fairly satisfied with your life.

Mostly 1s and 2s: Perhaps you should make changes in your life.

3 What does the term 'quality of life' mean to you? What factors are involved and how can we measure it? Brainstorm ideas in small groups.

4 Discuss the terms in the box. What do they mean? How can we measure them? Use a dictionary or other reference source if necessary.

| Standard of living | Gross national income | Gross national happiness |

5 **Read STUDY SKILL** 🎧 9.3 You are going to listen to the first part of the lecture on the Human Development Index (HDI).

1 Give a definition of HDI.

2 Make a note of the structure of the lecture. How many topics will there be? What are they?

3 What style of lecture is this, formal or informal? Give reasons for your view.

STUDY SKILL Recognizing lecture styles

Lecture styles vary greatly.

■ In some situations, lecturers are expected to be serious, maintain a formal atmosphere and use formal language.

■ In other situations, lecturers can be more informal, use less formal language and try to engage the audience by addressing them directly.

An informal style does not mean that the lecturer is not serious about the subject or that the topic is unimportant.

6 Read STUDY SKILL 🎧 9.4 Listen to the rest of the lecture and complete the information on the visuals.

1

HDI by country for year 2＿＿＿＿		
rank	country	HDI
1	Norway	0.938
2	＿＿＿＿＿＿＿	＿＿＿＿＿＿＿
3	＿＿＿＿＿＿＿	＿＿＿＿＿＿＿

STUDY SKILL
Getting the most out of visuals

To understand the data in visuals, read:
- the title of the visual.
- any headings in tables.
- information on the vertical and horizontal axes (bar charts and graphs).
- the key (colours, symbols, etc. used in the charts).

Try to see the overall pattern or trends in the data.

2

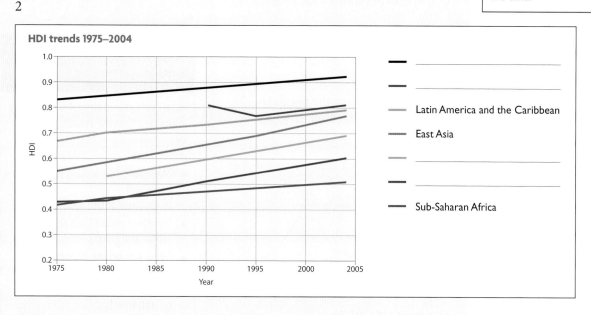

7 🎧 9.4 Listen again and answer the questions.
1 When was the Human Development Index launched?
2 What are the three dimensions to the HDI? Explain how they are measured.
3 What HDI do 'high development' countries have?
4 What are the predictions for the HDI in the future?
5 What are the three main criticisms of the HDI?
6 What alternative to HDI has been suggested?

8 Work in groups of three. Each student should study one of the graphs.
1 Explain the title and the information on the vertical and horizontal axes.
2 Give a short description of the data to the group.
3 Answer any questions the group may have.

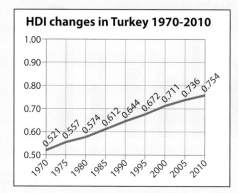

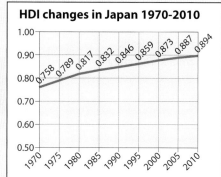

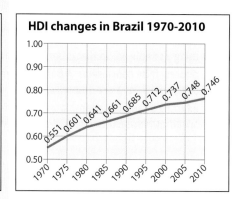

SPEAKING Presenting results

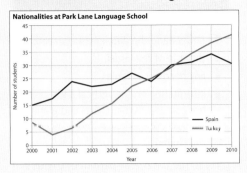

Nationalities at Park Lane Language School

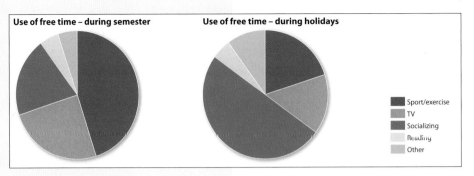

Use of free time – during semester

Use of free time – during holidays

- Sport/exercise
- TV
- Socializing
- Reading
- Other

1 Study the graph and the pie charts above. Discuss the questions with a partner.

1. What are the topics of the two studies?
2. How do you think these statistics were gathered?
3. How would you present the results?
4. What main points and overall trends would you focus on?

2 [Read STUDY SKILL] 🔊 9.5 Listen to two short reports. Which of the points in the Study Skills box do the speakers follow? Make notes and compare your answers with a partner.

3 [Read STUDY SKILL] 🔊 9.6 Listen to people describing the data below. In what way do they misrepresent the data?

1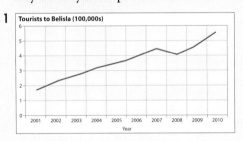
Tourists to Belisla (100,000s)

2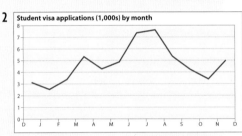
Student visa applications (1,000s) by month

3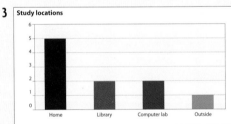
Study locations

4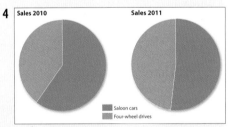
Sales 2010   Sales 2011
- Saloon cars
- Four-wheel drives

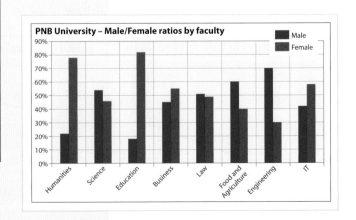
PNB University – Male/Female ratios by faculty
- Male
- Female

Humanities, Science, Education, Business, Law, Food and Agriculture, Engineering, IT

4 Look at the bar chart. Work in groups of four and discuss it. Describe the information.

Discussing a survey report

1 **Read STUDY SKILL** Look at these headings from a survey report on the use of ATMs or cash machines. What do you think should be included in each section? Discuss your ideas with a partner.

> Introduction   Method   Results
> Conclusions   Recommendations

2 🎧 **9.7** Listen to extracts from the four sections of a presentation on a survey.

1 What is the subject of the survey?
2 Decide which section of the presentation the extracts A–D are from.

☐ Introduction   ☐ Method   ☐ Results   ☐ Conclusion

3 🎧 **9.7** Listen to the extracts again and answer these questions on each section.

A 1 How was the study group chosen?
   2 Why did they choose a weekend?

B 1 What proportion of people would support a ban on smoking in malls?
   2 What was the alternative suggestion to a ban?

C 1 What proportion of the audience said they were disturbed by smoking?
   2 What did the speaker say about passive smoking?

D 1 What two visuals does the speaker refer to?
   2 What percentage of the survey group were smokers?

4 You are going to prepare a short presentation on the results of a survey. Use the information from the survey below.

> **Aim:** To find out about people moving to cities.
>
> **Method:** Telephone interviews with 200 people in the US and UK who have moved from rural addresses to urban addresses in the last three years.
>
> **Results:**
>
> | **Distance moved:** | **Job offer before the move:** |
> |---|---|
> | 22% under 20 miles | 43% yes |
> | 58% 20–200 miles | 48% no |
> | 20% over 200 miles | 9% no answer |
>
> | **Reason for move:** | **Satisfaction with move:** |
> |---|---|
> | 55% work | 37% satisfied |
> | 17% to be with family | 31% unsatisfied |
> | 11% access to services | 32% undecided |
> | 4% education | |
> | 13% other | |

1 Plan the talk. Use the headings from the Study Skill.
2 Prepare visuals to accompany each section of the talk, including the Results section.
3 Make sure the visuals used to show the data are clear and easy to understand.

5 Give your presentation to the rest of the class.

VOCABULARY DEVELOPMENT Multiple meanings

1 ■ Read STUDY SKILL Read the dictionary entries for the three words below. Choose which of the meanings is suitable for the word used in each sentence.

> ### STUDY SKILL Recognizing multiple meanings
>
> Many words in English have more than one meaning. These are listed in the dictionary beginning with the most common. For example: *resolution*
>
> **resolution** ⒶⓌ /ˌrezə'luːʃn/ *noun* **1** [U] the quality of being firm and determined **2** [U] solving or settling a problem, DISPUTE, etc. **3** [C] (POLITICS) a formal decision that is taken after a vote by a group of people: *The UN resolution condemned the invasion.* **4** [C] a firm decision to do or not to do sth **5** [U, sing.] (COMPUTING) the power of a computer screen, printer, etc. to give a clear image, depending on the size of the dots that make up the image: *high-resolution graphics*

faculty /'fæklti/ *noun* [C] (*pl.* **faculties**) **1** one of the natural abilities of a person's body or mind: *the faculty of hearing/sight/speech* **2** (*also* **Faculty**) (EDUCATION) one department in a university, college, etc.: *the Faculty of Law/Arts*

sector ☛⁰ ⒶⓌ /'sektə(r)/ *noun* [C] **1** a part of the business activity of a country: *The manufacturing sector has declined in recent years.* ↻ look at **the private sector, the public sector 2** a part of an area or of a large group of people: *the Christian sector of the city* **3** (MATHEMATICS) a part of a circle that is between two straight lines drawn from the centre to the edge ↻ picture at **circle**

trade¹ ☛⁰ /treɪd/ *noun* **1** [U] (ECONOMICS, SOCIAL STUDIES) the buying or selling of goods or services between people or countries: *an international trade agreement* ◇ *Trade is not very good (=not many goods are sold) at this time of year.* **2** [C] a particular type of business: *the tourist/building/retail trade* **3** [C,U] a job for which you need special skill, especially with your hands: *Jeff is a plumber by trade.* ◇ *to learn a trade* ↻ note at **work**

1 The agricultural **sector** of the economy has declined in recent years.
2 Many students want to go to university instead of learning a **trade** such as carpentry.
3 Sara was offered the position of Assistant Professor in the **Faculty** of Engineering.

2 Choose which of the meanings matches the bold word, according to the context. Use a dictionary to help you.

> 1 In 2003, about one-third of exports were to developing countries, but by 2009, this **proportion** had risen to nearly three quarters.
> • comparative part, share of a whole
> • the relationship between the parts and amount of two things
>
> 2 Developing countries **tend** to have higher population growth than developed ones.
> • to look after somebody or something
> • to usually do or be something
>
> 3 … and also more intelligent phones, so-called 'smart phones', that have computer-like **applications**: email, video-call facilities and so on.
> • a programme designed to do a particular job
> • a formal written request for a job or a place in a school, university, etc.
>
> 4 We will be looking at Internet **usage** throughout the world.
> • the way that something is used, the amount that something is used
> • the way that words are normally used in language
>
> 5 But as mobile phone ownership has become more **accessible**, so subscriptions have risen sharply.
> • possible to be reached or entered.
> • easy to get, use or understand.

sector

trade

faculty

3 The words below all have multiple meanings. Check the words in the dictionary and write a sentence for each, giving examples of two different meanings. For example, *draw* (v):

1 It is difficult to draw a conclusion as the survey was unreliable.
2 I can draw a map for you if you aren't sure of the location of the university.

panel (n)   effective (adj)   define (v)   index (n)   launch (v)

REVIEW

1 🎧 9.8 Listen to the lecturer. Choose which map is being referred to.

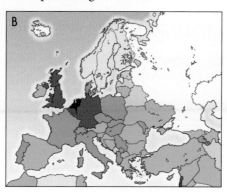

2 Read the statements below. Make changes so that the language is more tentative.

1 The price of oil will rise in the next few months.
2 People in Andorra live much longer than people in Russia.
3 Imports to the UK from China fell sharply last year. This was due to the recession in the UK.
4 Students spend more time in the library during the examination period than at other times of the year.
5 The survey shows that young people eat fast food at least twice a week.
6 Eating fast food causes obesity and heart disease in later life.

3 🎧 9.9 Listen to the speaker and correct the incorrect information on the slides.

1
Human Development Index
• Developed by United States
• Shows 'Standard of living'
• Is used to measure developing countries

2
The Netherlands
• Probability at birth of not surviving to age 60 (%) 6.7
• People lacking access to medical care (%) 7.5
• Long-term unemployment (%) 10.1

4 Work in pairs. Plan a presentation for the survey findings below.

Aim: To find out how much TV people watch in four different countries.
Method: Mailed surveys and in-person interviews (200 people in each country)
Results (television-watching hours-per-day by age)

	Under 14 years old	14–21	21–65	Over 65
Canada	2.8	3.3	1.3	3.7
Argentina	1.7	2.0	1.8	3.1
Egypt	2.0	2.6	2.1	2.1
Japan	2.5	2.7	1.1	1.1

10 Technological advances

LISTENING SKILLS Critical listening • Dealing with fast speech • Active listening: asking questions
• Pronunciation: homophones
SPEAKING SKILLS Recognizing an opposing view • Presentations (7) Delivery
VOCABULARY DEVELOPMENT Register (formal and informal)

LISTENING The end of books?

1 Look at photos of the devices on the right. Do you recognize any of them?
With a partner discuss the different ways they can be used.

2 Discuss the questions in groups and complete the table.

1 What are the advantages and disadvantages of books as a way of reading?
2 What are the advantages and disadvantages of e-books and e-readers?
3 Make lists of the main points. Use the expressions in the Language Bank
to give your opinion to the group – which do you prefer?

	advantages	disadvantages
Books		
E-books / E-readers		

LANGUAGE BANK Advantages and disadvantages

- *One advantage / disadvantage of (a book) is that …*
- *Another benefit / drawback is that …*
- *You can … a book, but you can't … an e-reader*
- *On the positive / negative side …*
- *On the one hand …, but on the other hand …*
- *I really prefer … because …*
- *The (advantages) are outweighed by the (disadvantages) …*
- *Overall I think the (advantages) are greater than the (disadvantages)*

---

3 🎧 10.1 You are going to listen to an extract from a radio documentary
Technology Input. Listen to the introduction to the programme and answer
the questions below.

1 Why is Chance Publishing in the news?
2 What things can be downloaded in addition to the book?
3 What is the main question the programme wants to answer?
4 Who is going to speak next in the programme?

4 **Read STUDY SKILL** 🔊 10.2 Listen to an extract from the radio documentary. Discuss the questions in groups.

1 What are the views of the publisher?
2 What reasons does he give to support these views?
3 Does he give any evidence?
4 What is his main conclusion?
5 In general, do you think he gives a strong argument in support of e-books?

STUDY SKILL Critical listening

When someone presents their views in an interview or talk, try to evaluate the argument they are using. As you listen try to:
- identify the speaker's views.
- look for reasons.
- evaluate evidence.
- evaluate conclusions.

Speakers often signal the conclusions of their arguments by markers such as:
therefore, as a result, so, consequently

In this way we can follow the argument and judge its strength or weakness. It helps us to present other views or counter-arguments.

5 🔊 10.2 Listen again and answer the questions.

1 What two things are new about the service the publisher is offering?
2 Why does he think the reading experience using e-readers is more rewarding?
3 Does he think that all people will prefer e-books?
4 How does he think e-books and e-readers can be useful at work or at home?
5 What does he think about 'glare' from screens?
6 Why does he think the music industry made a mistake?
7 What does he think the publishing industry should do about the new technology?
8 What will happen to the market for reading?

6 In the table below are some arguments that an author is using against e-books and e-readers. Match the reasons with the conclusions using a linking phrase.

reasons		conclusions
1 People will download e-books illegally.	Therefore …	a the reader may be distracted from the content of the book.
2 Glare from a screen can hurt the eyes.	As a result …	b people do not like reading in this way.
3 E-books also contain videos, music, games, etc.	So …	c the reader can only use them for a few hours at a time.
4 E-readers need a source of power.	Consequently …	d they will not need to buy traditional books.

7 Discuss the conclusions from exercise 6 in pairs. Do you agree or disagree? Can you come to any other conclusions about e-books? What are your reasons?

Technology of the future

1 How do you think technology will develop in the future? Discuss with a partner, with reference to the words in the box.

mobile phones	TV sets	electric cars	the Internet	computers

2 Study the terms below. What do you think the terms mean? Discuss with a partner. Use a dictionary or the Internet to help.

- solar fuel
- **social television**
- **green concrete**
- implantable electronics
- **real-term search**

solar

green

change

3 🎧 10.3 Listen to this introduction to lecture on emerging technologies and answer the questions.

  1 How does *Technology Review* choose the most important emerging technologies?

  2 What examples are given of 'large-scale changes'?

  3 Are all of the changes large scale? What other types of change are there?

  4 What medical example is given?

4 **Read STUDY SKILL** 🎧 10.4 Listen to extracts from the introduction. Try to identify the content words and underline them. The first is done as an example.

  1 The <u>winners</u> are chosen by the <u>editors</u> to cover <u>key fields</u>. The <u>question</u> we ask is <u>simple</u>: is the <u>technology</u> likely to <u>change</u> the <u>world</u>?

  2 Some of these changes are on the largest possible scale: better bio-fuels, more efficient solar cells and green concrete all aim to tackle global warming in the years ahead.

  3 Other changes are more local and involve how we use technology: for example, 3D screens on mobile devices, new applications for cloud computing and social television.

  4 What I'd like to do in today's lecture, the last in this semester on Technology, is to briefly review five of the selected technologies – new technologies that may become important in the near future.

  5 The five examples we have selected come from five different fields – from communication, construction, medicine, science and lastly the media.

STUDY SKILL Dealing with fast speech

Some lecturers and presenters speak quickly. Listeners can adopt some strategies to help.

Before the lecture:
- prepare even more carefully and read about the topic.
- ask for permission to record the lecture.

During the lecture:
- focus on the stressed, content words in the sentence.
- take notes using abbreviations and symbols where you can.
- listen for signal words and clues to important information.

After the lecture:
- check your notes with those of other students.
- study any hand-outs from the lecture.

5 `Read STUDY SKILL` The following are examples of good questions for a lecture. What type of questions are they? Match the questions with the four types in the study skill.

1 Some people say that solar fuel is the way forward. What's your view on this?
2 I didn't quite catch what you said about streaming data. Could you go over it again?
3 You mentioned 'cloud computing' earlier on. What is that exactly?
4 I was interested to hear that silk can be used for medical implants. I wonder if you could give us some more examples of how silk is used for medical purposes?

6 🎧 10.5 Listen to the lecture and write notes on each type of technology.

7 🎧 10.5 Use your notes from exercise 6 to say if the following sentences are True (T) or False (F). Correct the false statements. Then listen again and check your answers.

1 Streams can be defined as continuous data.
2 Solar fuel comes from crops such as corn.
3 Carbon dioxide is generated by the production of cement for concrete.
4 Green concrete takes in carbon dioxide during the production process.
5 Implants are small electronic devices that are placed inside the body.
6 Implants made of silk have to be removed after a few years.
7 TV viewing is becoming more popular around the world.
8 Social TV combines social networking with TV.

8 Write five questions you would like to ask the lecturer. Use different types of question. Compare your questions with a partner.

9 `Read STUDY SKILL` 🎧 10.6 Listen and complete the sentences with the correct form of the words you hear.

1 Our course starts next _____ and ends in January.
2 The results showed that Osman was rather _____ in Maths and Physics.
3 A note was made of the _____ of the substance before and after heating.
4 The committee decided to _____ for the report before making a decision.
5 The airport terminal was constructed using mainly glass and _____ .
6 If a student plagiarizes a text then they really _____ the author's ideas.
7 The _____ aim of the presentation is to outline changes in book technology.
8 An important _____ of chemistry is that it is better to prevent waste than to clean it up afterwards.
9 The _____ of the new airport will be decided by the government next year.
10 The _____ of so many people in the crowded shopping mall made Sami feel claustrophobic.

STUDY SKILL
Active listening: asking questions

It's important to listen actively. Do this by asking questions for:
■ clarification
■ repetition
■ further information
■ opinion

STUDY SKILL
Pronunciation: homophones

Homophones are words which sound the same but have different meanings, and usually different spellings. Common examples are:
here/hear made/maid peace/piece their/there/they're wear/where

SPEAKING   Giving and supporting opinions

1 Imagine that all the textbooks you need for your course of study are available on an e-reader. Would you choose to buy one, or would you prefer to use books? Discuss your ideas with a partner.

2 ☒ **Read STUDY SKILL** 💿 10.7 Listen to two speakers giving their opinions of e-readers. Answer the questions.

1 Which speaker presents the best argument?
2 Why is this speaker's argument the best?
3 What are the weaknesses in the other speaker's argument?

3 Read the statements below. How would you support these arguments by recognizing the opposing view? Work with a partner and use expressions from the Language Bank. For example:

'Smoking in public should be banned.'

It's true that personal freedoms are important. However, I feel that smoking in public should be banned.

1 Public transport should be free in cities.
2 Children should be given jobs to do in the home.
3 The Internet is harmful for children.
4 Mobile phones are the most important invention of the last fifty years.

> **LANGUAGE BANK** Building an argument
>
> | Supporting an argument: | Recognizing the opposite view: |
> |---|---|
> | *Research seems to indicate …* | *I agree that … but …* |
> | *A recent survey showed …* | *I admit that …* |
> | *According to a study by X, …* | *It is true that …* |
> | *An example of … is …* | |

4 You are going to discuss the benefits of new technologies. Work in small groups and follow the stages.

1 Each person should choose one of the following topics:

> • **Facebook**   • **Plastic surgery**   • **3D films**
>
> • **Laptop computers**   • **Mobile phones**

2 Research information on the topic.
3 Prepare to give your opinions on the topic. Find ways to support your point of view, for example:

Social networking sites such as Facebook can be dangerous. For example, there are many examples of personal information being used …

Also consider views opposing your own:

Many people say they are a wonderful way for people to get in touch with others …

5 Present your views to the rest of your group. Give a short (two-minute) account of your views to the group. Be prepared to answer any questions they may have.

> **STUDY SKILL**
> **Recognizing an opposing view**
>
> One way to strengthen your argument in a discussion or debate is to recognize the opposing view. This shows that you:
>
> - are an open-minded person.
> - have spent time thinking about the issue deeply.
> - have looked at all sides of the argument.
> - have considered the alternatives to your point of view and rejected them.
>
> Make sure you support your argument further by saying why you disagree with the opposing arguments.

Giving a presentation on new technology

1 Imagine that you have to give a presentation about a tablet computer or a similar piece of technology. Work with a partner. Decide how you would structure the presentation. What headings would you use?

2 **Read STUDY SKILL** 🔘 10.8 Listen to introductions to three presentations. Decide which presentation is best and how could they each be improved.

3 Look at the pictures of presenters. Match the presenter with the advice about body language in the Study Skill box.

> ### STUDY SKILL
> ### Presentations (7) Delivery
>
> Delivery is an important presentation skill. For example speakers should:
> - speak clearly and confidently.
> - speak loudly enough for everyone to hear.
> - use an appropriate level of language and content for the audience.
> - face the audience.
> - make eye contact with people in the audience.
>
> Speakers should not:
> - turn their backs on the audience.
> - use too many hand gestures.
> - move around unnecessarily.
> - cross their arms or legs.
> - read from notes.
> - speak too quickly.

4 You are going to give a presentation on a new piece of technology. In pairs, decide which new technology you are going to use.

1 Plan the structure of your presentation.
- Introduction
- Description / history of the technology
- Features / uses
- Evaluation – will it be successful?
- Conclusion
2 Prepare visuals for the presentation.
3 Make sure you follow the points in the checklist.

Presentation checklist
• Plan the presentation in advance.
• Make sure there is a good introduction and conclusion.
• Use a logical structure (chronological, cause-effect, etc.).
• Use content and language appropriate to the audience.
• Provide clear, concise visuals where necessary.
• Introduce yourself to the audience.
• Deliver the presentation clearly and use appropriate body language.
• Establish rapport with the audience.
• Keep to the time limits.

5 Give your presentation to the class. Follow all of the guidelines regarding delivery and body language.

VOCABULARY DEVELOPMENT Register

1 `Read STUDY SKILL` Look at the following extract from the first part of a fairly informal talk. Choose the more formal options.

Today ¹**I'm going to/I intend** *to* discuss the ²**various/different** problems associated with book publishing. First I will ³**present/give** an overview of trends in book publishing over the last ⁴**couple of/two hundred** years. Then I'll ⁵**talk about/discuss** recent trends in book publishing, and finally I'll ⁶**attempt/try** to make predictions about the future of publishing.

OK, I'll begin by ⁷**looking at/examining** how the book has ⁸**evolved/changed** since the 19ᵗʰ century. Of course, we have to ⁹**think about/consider** the question of literacy. In Britain in the 19ᵗʰ century, for example, not everyone was literate. In 1841 ¹⁰**approximately/about** a third of the male population and 44% of the female population were not able to write their names. ¹¹**However/But** with the spread of schooling, literacy rates continued to ¹²**go up/rise** during the ¹³**remainder/rest** of the century.

STUDY SKILL Register (formal and informal)

Lectures can be formal or informal. However, to sound more academic, and more serious, it is better to use formal language.

One of the main features of style is the choice of vocabulary. Many common informal words and phrases in English have a formal equivalent, e.g.

| *buy / purchase* | *talk / discuss* | *look at / examine* |
| *find out / discover* | *would like to / intend to* | *lots of / a large number of* |

2 Read the sentences. Try to make the style more formal by replacing the word or phrases in bold with more formal vocabulary. Use a dictionary to help.

1 Sales of tea in the UK have **gone down** steadily over the last few years. This is due mainly to the popularity of coffee as an alternative **drink**.

2 Evidence shows that **eating** fast food on a regular basis causes young people to become **very fat**.

3 The participants were **picked** for the study on the basis of their level of education.

4 The solution was **put** in a glass container and heated gently until a change in colour was **seen**.

5 Photosynthesis is a process where sunlight is **taken in** by plants. The sun's energy is then used to **change** carbon dioxide in the air into proteins.

6 Consumers can **buy** these devices in e-shops.

7 **Also**, it is important to **think about** the effect that this process has on the environment.

REVIEW

1 🎧 10.9 Listen to the speaker and choose the correct answer.

1 The speaker discusses changes in how films are **made / distributed**.
2 People stopped using VHS because **the VHS shops closed / they were lower quality than DVDs**.
3 Video streaming is when you **watch films online / receive films in the post**.
4 The speaker believes there will be **fewer / more** DVDs in the future.

2 🎧 10.9 Listen again and answer the questions.

1 Why does the speaker believe that DVD rental chains have closed?
2 Why does the speaker believe mail rental services will become less popular?
3 What new technology has led to online streaming?
4 Why does the speaker believe that online streaming will be popular with consumers?

3 Work with a partner and write three questions you would like to ask the speaker.

4 Discuss topics 1–6 with a partner. Try to use the phrases in the box.

1 green concrete
2 solar fuel
3 social TV
4 implantable electronics
5 real-time search
6 traditional books

> Research seems to indicate …
> A recent survey showed …
> An example of … is …
> According to a study by X …
> I agree that … but …
> I admit that …
> It is true that …

5 Rewrite the informal sentences to make them more formal. Use the words in the box.

however	examined	purchase	intend	progressed

1 Consumers are eager to buy the newest technological devices available.
2 The researchers want to demonstrate that e-readers are as easy to use as traditional books.
3 I agree with most of your argument, but I'd like to clarify a few points.
4 The company's developers have looked at new possibilities in telecommunications.
5 Internet retail has moved so quickly that many traditional shops have had difficulties staying up-to-date.

AUDIO SCRIPTS

 1.1

I want to talk to you today about how you can prepare for life at university and how you can become a successful student. It's not always easy to do, but later on I'll give you some tips – some dos and don'ts – to help you be successful. First of all, I want to define success. Success doesn't mean being better than everyone else. Success means being the best you can be, but not everyone can get top marks all of the time. There will be students who get top marks in your group – you may be one yourself – but don't waste time competing with other people. The only person you should compete with is yourself. Try to improve on what you did last time. This requires a very important quality – motivation.

Where does motivation come from? That's up to you to find out. Sometimes it's external – from outside – pressure from parents, your peers, your lecturers, from exams. But the best kind of motivation comes from yourself – from inside. By the end of the course or study programme, don't be one of those students who says, 'I wish I'd worked harder.' Even if you failed you should be able to say to yourself: 'I did the best I could'.

1.2

Now I'd like to turn to some practical points. Firstly, let's deal with the things that you should do. One of the most important skills is being able to manage your time – time management. Make a study plan – so you know when you have lectures and when you have time to study – to do assignments, read, and research on the Internet. But don't forget to put aside time for relaxation, exercise, and entertainment. These are important too.

Following on from that, another piece of advice is to meet deadlines. If you have an assignment to do for example – plan your time and start working on it as soon as you can so that you meet the deadline. Don't leave everything to the last minute.

The next bit of advice concerns resources. You should organize the resources you need. During your studies you will need to have access to a lot of information. Where are you going to get this information from? What resources do you have? By resources I mean course books, reference books, dictionaries, and so on – as well as libraries and the Internet. Keeping track of your resources will help you be more efficient in your studies.

Another important resource is people. Find out which people are available – your lecturers, tutors, the librarians. Get to know them and find out when they're available to talk to. Don't forget your fellow students. Form a study group! Not everyone likes to work with other people, but working with other students in a study group can be a useful way of sharing information – and it can be motivating too.

The final point is to find out your strengths and weaknesses. What are you good at? What are you not so good at? We can call this self-assessment. If you know that your weaknesses are, for example, taking part in discussions, or completing work on time, then you can take steps to improve that.

Finally I'd like to deal with some of the 'don'ts'. Things that good students should not do …

1.3

Today I'd like to speak about intelligence. First, I'd like to discuss how intelligence is measured, because, I think that this is a good place to begin to think about how we define the term. I'll begin with a brief history of intelligence testing.

The traditional view of intelligence was based around the IQ test. IQ stands for intelligence quotient. Quotient just means number – a way of measuring intelligence. It was devised in 1912 by the German psychologist William Stern. It was a way of measuring children's intelligence.

Nowadays it's used to measure the performance of both adults and children. The IQ score is a prediction of where the individual is compared to other people. Have a look at this graph. It shows the distribution of IQ amongst the population in general. The horizontal axis – here – shows IQ scores ranging from 40 here on the left – to 160 on the right. The vertical axis shows the percentage of people who have that IQ score – it ranges from 0% to over 2.5%. Now, you can see from this curve that the average IQ is 100 – represented here as the highest part of the curve. So just over 2.5% of the population have an average IQ. There are fewer people with IQs over 110, 120, and so on, and very few with IQs over 140. At the other extreme – here – you can see, similarly, that few people have IQs of less than 80 for example, and very few less than 60. What does the shape of the graph remind you of? Yes that's right – a bell. The shape of the graph is like a bell – and that's the reason it's known as a 'bell curve'.

However, many people think that this view of intelligence is very limited …

1.4

Now let's move on to multiple intelligences. This theory was developed in 1983 by Howard Gardner, a professor of Education at Harvard University. He said that the traditional idea of intelligence was far too limited. He believes there are at least seven different intelligences. These intelligences describe the potential in children and adults – what people are able to do. If you look at this table you can see that the seven intelligences are listed in this column and here on the right are their main features – what a person is able to do if they score highly in this type of intelligence. I'll go through the intelligences one by one.

Firstly, there is linguistic intelligence. Basically, linguistic intelligence means being able to use words well – in speaking, reading, writing, and so on. Such a person might speak several languages or be a good presenter.

Next, logical-mathematical intelligence. A person with good logical-mathematical intelligence is good with numbers, and they can deal with scientific or legal problems easily. Some people say that traditional intelligence tests, the IQ test for example, mainly focus on just this type of intelligence.

The third type of intelligence is spatial intelligence. The word 'spatial' involves area or space, for example, being able to use maps and plans effectively – maps in navigation – finding out where you are and where you are going, and plans in architecture – plans of buildings, and so on.

Let's move onto the fourth type of intelligence. This is called bodily-kinaesthetic intelligence. 'Kinaesthetic' means movement – so this intelligence refers to movement of the body. People with good bodily-kinaesthetic intelligence are good at sports, or drama, or dancing. Or they might be good at making things with their hands, such as models.

The fifth type is musical intelligence. Such a person may be good at singing, or composing music, or playing a musical instrument.

The last two are interpersonal and *intra*personal intelligences. Let me explain these terms carefully – they sound rather similar. Interpersonal intelligence means 'between people', a person who is good at communicating with others. Someone who is good at understanding other people and dealing with their problems – they may also be good at teaching. Intrapersonal, however, means 'within' a person – refers to a person who understands himself or herself, who is good at self-management, and capable of reflection, thinking about what they're doing about their life, and their goals.

1.5

Now I'd like to deal with the implications of this theory. If we accept Gardner's theory, that there are in fact seven intelligences and not just one generalized intelligence, what does this mean? What are the implications?

Gardner says that our schools and colleges focus most of their attention on just two types – linguistic intelligence, that's language, and logical-mathematical intelligence. In addition to this, he says, we should focus attention on the other intelligences as well, providing for students who are gifted in other ways – in music, design, therapy, as some examples.

This leads to a further conclusion – that teachers should teach in a variety of ways. Why? Because this would use all of the intelligences. For example, a teacher shouldn't just rely on lectures, worksheets, and textbooks. They should employ other methods of teaching in the lessons such as using music, or acting, taking the students on field trips, and using cooperative or group learning.

 1.6

A = Andrew   S = Sarah

A Hi, Sarah. What are you studying?

S Economics. We have a test tomorrow.

A Oh, good luck!

S I'm going to need it! I always leave revision to the last minute. You remember we had that talk last week about study habits – strengths and weaknesses and so on?

A Yes.

S Well that's one of my main weaknesses, I think – leaving revision right to the end.

A I can't meet deadlines, that's my big problem. I'm always late with assignments. But I am good at giving presentations. I enjoy talking to people – explaining things. That's one of my strengths, I think.

S I like talking too, but not presentations. I prefer discussing with people. I think I perform well in seminar discussions.

A Do you always work here in the library?

S Yeah, I usually sit at the same desk and bring all my books and my laptop. I like to work here in the evenings after lectures – it's quieter then.

A Oh I like the mornings. I get up about 6 and work for a couple of hours before breakfast. I prefer working at home – in my room. I have everything there and I can take breaks when I want – and have a cup of coffee.

S Yeah, I think it's important to take breaks. I usually take one every hour.

A I see you have a lot of notes there, I never take notes. I find it slows me down!

S Oh no, I think taking notes is important. It helps me to concentrate while I'm reading – and then I can use the notes later. In that talk the speaker said time management was important. What about that? Do you plan your week?

A Not really. I don't have a study plan – maybe I should.

S I don't have one either. But I agree they are a good idea.

A Sarah, do you always like to work on your own? I think it's a bit lonely here in the library. I like to work with other people. I belong to a kind of study group, you know.

S A study group? No, I prefer to work alone. I find if I work with other people they always want to chat about other things so I can't concentrate properly!

A Oh I see. In that case I had better go and let you work.

S OK. See you later.

 1.7

P = Peter   S = Stefan   K = Katrina

P I'm not sure these so-called 'intelligences' are in fact intelligences at all. Take musical intelligence as an example. My cousin is very good at the piano, but I would call this a skill not intelligence. What do you think, Stefan?

S Well, Peter, if you say that intelligence is only mathematical intelligence or logical intelligence then very few people can be called intelligent, but in fact …

K Yes, but …

S Could I just finish? In fact, we see people all around us who are good at certain things – like learning languages or reading maps. I would call these types of people intelligent too. Now I'm not so sure about bodily-kinaesthetic intelligence. Here I think we are talking about skills or talent and not intelligence.

K I'd like to make a point here. I disagree about people who make things with their hands or who are good at sports – bodily-kinaesthetic intelligence. I do think this is a kind of intelligence. Take footballers for example.

P I wouldn't say footballers are very intelligent. It seems to me …

K Well, let me explain. I think it does take a lot of intelligence to pass a football at the right angle and the right speed so that another player can receive the ball. And scoring goals too – that takes intelligence – judging the distance and the position of the goalkeeper. This is a type of intelligence. Don't you agree, Peter?

P No Katrina I don't agree at all. I think we can say footballers are very fit and also they are skilled in some ways, but …

 1.8

My name's Maria. I'm a few weeks into my second year of uni. I'm doing a degree in Engineering. I'm really happy with the course. The lecturers are great, which is obviously motivating, and, well, I really love Engineering so I'm finding it all really engaging. I got good marks in all of my modules last year and I think I am a pretty good student. I don't know if I'll end up with a distinction, but I'm pretty sure I'll be near the top of my class.

There is a lot of work to do. I feel like we've just got back and I already had a presentation last week and I've got to hand in a research paper on Friday. But like I said, I don't mind the work. In fact I enjoy it. I'm in the library most evenings and I try to start my assignments well in advance of the deadlines. It's easy to be motivated when you're really interested in the material.

 1.9

This graph shows the number of international students enrolled at this university by year. And as you can see on the graph the number of international students at this University has been increasing since the mid-1990s. The horizontal axis shows the year. The first year on the graph is 1995 and it goes up to 2009 over here. The vertical axis shows the total number of international students enrolled. You can see back in 1995, it was only 129. In 1996, that figure rose to 140. But then if we look over here, in the year 2000, it jumps to over 280. That figure steadily increases – see here 2004, 2006 – until it peaked in 2007. In 2008, there were slightly fewer, possibly due to the onset of the global financial crisis, but we expect these numbers to go up again within the next couple of years.

 2.1

I'll just give a brief summary of a few of the therapies that we're going to discuss today.

One that you might be familiar with is acupuncture. Acupuncture involves inserting needles into specific points in the body and manipulating them. It's used to relieve pain and to treat certain conditions.

And you've probably also heard of herbal medicine, which involves treatments using plants and plant extracts – a sort of natural alternative to conventional pharmaceuticals.

Has anyone heard of hydrotherapy? This is a therapy which uses water to treat illnesses or relieve pain. Water jets, mineral baths, and underwater massage are common examples.

Moving along, I think hypnosis is a very interesting therapy. What happens is a patient is put into an almost sleep-like condition and in this condition they are open to suggestions. As a result, the hypnotherapist can help them modify behaviours relating to health, stress or pain management.

The last therapy we'll discuss is yoga, which some of you might recognize as a type of exercise, but it's actually used as a therapy as well. This involves holding the body in different positions. It's often used to treat high blood pressure, insomnia and digestive problems, among other things.

2.2

L = Lee   S = Sunil   M = Miriam

M Who's going to begin our discussion? Sunil, how about you?

S Thank you, Miriam. Well, it seems to me that in the lecture, Dr Hall was basically saying that alternative medicine doesn't really exist. He said that alternative medicine was not real medicine as it was unproven – and we should only consider scientific, or evidence-based medicine.

M Yes, he claimed that only conventional medicine was based on proper scientific research.

S He seemed to be saying that as there is no real evidence for so-called alternative medicine –claims made by alternative therapists should be treated with caution. What are your feelings about this? Miriam?

M Generally speaking, I feel that Dr Hall's right – none of the alternative treatments have had proper scientific tests and shouldn't be considered medicine at all. Do you disagree, Lee?

L Well, there is plenty of evidence for alternative medicine. For example, a couple of years ago my aunt was suffering from a serious illness. She went to several conventional doctors and they could do nothing for her.

M I'm sorry to interrupt, Lee. But that is not scientific evidence – it's anecdotal evidence. Dr Hall talked about this.

L What do you mean by anecdotal?

M Well, with respect, this is a personal story about what happened to your aunt. That doesn't count as evidence, not scientific evidence anyway.

L But it's a true story and she was cured. She's fine now and conventional medicine didn't work at all. She tried everything. Finally she tried homeopathic medicine which was recommended to her and within a few weeks she completely recovered. It was remarkable.

M But I don't think that we can say for sure that it was homeopathic medicine that cured your aunt. It could have been some other factor that cured her.

L No. We tried everything as I said. The homeopathic medicine worked.

S Actually, I agree with Lee – to a point. There does seem to be an awful lot of what you call anecdotal evidence that some of these treatments work and if you have enough anecdotal evidence then, well, something must be going on. Look at Chinese medicine, for example.

L That's right. Chinese medicine has been around for a very long time – thousands of years in the case of acupuncture, for example. These treatments must work if they have been used for so long.

M I take your point, Lee. These treatments may seem to work, but is that real evidence? We have to be sure that it is not just chance. That's why proper scientific tests are important to find correlations and to prove that there is a link between cause and effect.

S Well, I think we should keep an open mind – at least until we have the scientific evidence.

L I think we do have the evidence, Sunil. For example, tests on diabetes patients in the US showed a strong correlation between herbal treatment and improvement in their condition.

S It seems to me that all other treatments – conventional medicines – have had proper scientific tests – and they are proven, whereas alternative medicines haven't been properly tested. So I suppose Dr Hall is right when he says we should be careful. But on the other hand that doesn't mean to say that alternatives therapies don't work.

M Well, I tend to agree with Dr Hall. We need evidence.

L Miriam, you always agree with Dr Hall!

M No, I don't. I didn't agree last week when he said that my report was not up to standard.

2.3

B = Bill   M = Mary   D = Don   F = Flavia

B Hello. Welcome to Scientific Research – our weekly podcast looking at what's new in the world of science. This week we are looking at the results of an interesting survey on students' academic performance and how it may be related to … the amount of exercise they get. Yes, that's right – exercise! Does this really mean students should be in the gym instead of the library? Mary Thomas investigates …

M I'm in the library at Manchester University in the north of England. There are lots of students sitting at desks – some at computer screens – and some have been here for hours. All in all it would seem that studying is not a very healthy pursuit. Add to that the fact that many students, because they are away from home, live on very poor diets. You could conclude that studying is not an active or healthy pastime. But now new research suggests that it may also have a much wider effect. Let me explain.

2.4 [including 2.5]

B = Bill   M = Mary   D = Don   F = Flavia

[2.5 starts] **M** A study carried out by Dr William McCarthy and colleagues at the University of California in Los Angeles came up with some pretty interesting results. They compared the physical fitness and body weight of students with their scores in Maths, reading and language tests. Altogether they tested nearly 2,000 students between the years 2002 and 2003. About half were female and half male. They were all from different ethnic backgrounds.

First they weighed the students and found that almost 32% were overweight. Then they tested their fitness by asking them to walk or run for one mile. They noted the time they took to complete the mile. The boys averaged just under 10 minutes and the girls 11 minutes to complete the course. Amazingly, 65% of the students were below the California state fitness standard.

Now when these results were matched with the test results what did they find? Well, they found that the students who were fit had higher test scores than those who were not fit. And it was the same picture for the weight of the students. Those students who had a desirable weight scored higher on the tests than those who were overweight. It seems to show a correlation between fitness and high grades – in other words, exercise is beneficial for academic performance. But a note of caution, researchers say they are not really sure why this is the case. [2.5 ends]

Let's get the views of some university students in Manchester. I'm here now in the sports centre in Manchester University. It's eight o'clock in the morning and as you can see it is already very busy. I'm going to speak to a couple of students who are working out on the cycling machines. Don, can you tell me how often you come to the gym?

D About twice a week – more if I can. It depends on the workload.

M What do you think of this research that says you may get better grades if you exercise? Is it working for you?

D I'm not sure it's working yet in my case!

M OK, well good luck! I have Flavia here now. Where are you from Flavia, and what are you studying?

F I'm from Brazil – São Paulo – and I'm studying Urban Planning.

M And what do you think about exercise – how does it help you?

F Well, I come here almost every day and I work out for about an hour. I really think it helps me. I usually feel very relaxed afterwards and more alert mentally when I go to lectures later in the day.

M And does it help with your grades?

F Well, I think it has done – so far!

M Well, it seems to be working with those students anyhow. Back to you, Bill.

B Thanks, Mary. Well, that's all for this week's podcast. Remember there's more information about this topic on our university website.

2.6

1 Today we've been looking at research into diet and health and I've outlined some of the major studies that have been carried out in recent years in countries like Japan, the USA and in India. I think it is quite clear from the results of these studies that there is a clear link between …

2 What I'd like to do today is to see if there is a correlation between what we eat and our general health. In particular, I want to look at the link between the consumption of meat and diseases such as cancer. I think this is an important area of study because …

3 Next, I would like to look at the results of a study that was carried out in Japan in 2009. More than five thousand people were interviewed about their eating habits. Now as you know, Japan is mainly a fish-eating society. But increasingly the Japanese, especially the young people in Japan …

4 I'll try to leave ten minutes or so for questions at the end of the presentation, but if anything is not clear please feel free to interrupt me at any time …

5 What we need are more large-scale studies of the type I have mentioned. Hopefully, in the future such studies will lead to a greater understanding of diseases such as cancer and help us in our efforts to find effective treatment …

2.7

Hello. My name's Francesco Mancini. I work for the organization, World Health International. Today I'd like to talk about one particular part of health-care and that is alternative or complementary medicine. Perhaps I'd better start by explaining what these terms mean. 'Alternative' is used by people who want to show that their approach to medicine is different from conventional medicine – an example would be acupuncture. 'Complementary' means that approaches such as acupuncture can be used alongside conventional medicine. Now why should we be talking about alternative medicine? One of the main reasons is the growing interest we have seen in this approach to medicine, especially in the western world. The aim of this talk is to answer this question: Should we take alternative therapies seriously? I'll begin with a brief review of the history of alternative therapies and their growth in recent years. Then I'd like to describe a few of these approaches in detail – what they are and what they claim to do. And finally, I'll be examining some of the evidence. By the way, if you have any questions, there will be five minutes or so at the end of the talk for discussion.

2.8

P = Phil   R = Roberta   G = Gemma

P OK, well the question is whether or not a healthy and nutritious diet contributes to academic success. I think this is a complicated issue and I'm not sure where to start with it. What do you think, Roberta?

R Well actually, Phil, I think it's quite obvious that it does. Successful students use a lot of energy when they're researching, studying and preparing presentations. They need to be wide awake and focused to do these things well. We've just read an article from a medical journal, which explained that students should make sure they get enough protein, because protein provides the energy that the brain requires. So I think students need to eat healthy food to provide them with sufficient protein and energy. Hmmm. You look like you disagree, Gemma.

G I think you have a valid point, Roberta, when you say that students need to get enough energy. However, I'm not so sure that the evidence indicates that this energy has to come from a healthy diet. There are many sources of energy available to students, which probably aren't considered 'healthy' by most people. I mean sugary foods and caffeinated drinks can provide energy, but these aren't healthy, are they?

P This is exactly what I meant when I said that this issue is more complex than it appears at first glance. I don't know if we have enough evidence to conclusively say one way or the other.

G I don't know, Phil. I think it's pretty clear that many students are both unhealthy and successful. We've seen a study which shows that students are eating more junk food than they did in the past. We also know that the number of university graduates has increased by five percent in the past two years. I think this shows that a healthy diet is not necessary for academic achievement.

R I'm sorry, Gemma, but I don't think you can draw that conclusion from …

2.9

We know that therapies involving water or baths have existed since ancient times. They were used by the ancient Greeks, Romans, Chinese and probably others. However, modern hydrotherapy can be traced back to the 19th century, when it was reintroduced by a monk, Father Sebastian Kneipp, who lived in Bavaria, in what is now Germany. His idea, that water can be used to cure people, caught on across Europe, and is still a widely-practised treatment today.

So how does it work? Well, one way hydrotherapy works is it uses the body's reaction to hot and cold to stimulate the immune system or produce beneficial relaxing effects that reduce harmful stress and anxiety. Another way that hydrotherapy is used to heal is through baths: steam baths and saunas. Toxins can be drawn out of the body through sweating and other processes.

Hydrotherapy is commonly used as a therapy for back pain. It can also be effective for anxiety, insomnia, and arthritis.

3.1

P = Presenter   M = Martin Holt

P London is undeniably a global metropolis. It's the ninth largest city on the planet and its citizens speak over 300 different languages. It has an economy roughly the size of Sweden's. But how did it become the city that it is today? On this week's podcast, I'll be discussing this question with social historian Martin Holt. Welcome, Martin. So, to start, could you talk about how the city we know today came to be?

M Well, from the time that it was founded in the first century by the Romans, London has always been an important trading city, mostly because of its location on the Thames. And by the late Middle Ages it had grown into a trading capital. The Royal Exchange, where merchants could buy and sell goods, was opened in 1571.

P Well, when you walk through London today, it doesn't look like a mediaeval city.

M There are several reasons for this. You see, in 1666 the Great Fire of London destroyed the mediaeval city. Over 80% of all homes in the city were lost in the fire. However, the fire provided a clean slate upon which the city could be rebuilt. As people from rural areas migrated to London, a new city grew to accommodate them all.

P Sorry, but could you explain why so many people wanted to move to London at this time?

M To find work. The Agricultural Revolution in the 1700s increased the country's production of food enormously – and this made it possible to support large cities. At the same time, the new efficient farming methods and machines required many fewer farmworkers.

P Which meant large numbers of unemployed workers in the countryside?

M Precisely. Many of these people were forced to leave the countryside to find work in cities. London was the centre of commerce and industry for the newly developing British Empire, so there were people coming in from all over the world. By the year 1800, the population of London had grown to just under a million – an enormous city for that time. By the end of that century the population had shot up to over 6.5 million.

P So, you were explaining how this influx of newcomers changed the city?

M The huge changes started to occur back in the 18th century with the construction of roads and bridges. Until 1714, there was still only one bridge across the Thames in London. The growth of basic infrastructure allowed the city to expand. The rich and middle classes built squares for housing development mostly to the west of the old city. The clerks and lower-middle class workers had houses further out in the suburbs. The poor lived in brick terrace slums towards the east of the city. Soon, the centre of the original city was no longer residential – it had become the financial centre.

P So people had to travel further to get to work.

M Exactly. The development of London's public transport system was crucial to its development as a city. First, there were omnibuses drawn by horses – from 1829. However, they were too expensive for the average worker. The poor walked, which meant the streets were often congested with pedestrians. The author H G Wells described the crowds in London as 'a great mysterious movement of unaccountable beings'.

P That does sound like London.

M Euston station, the first railway station in London, opened in 1837. People could live further from the centre where they worked. And more workers were needed at this time specifically for projects such as building the railways. This happened again in the 1860s with the construction of the London Underground, the Tube, the first underground system in the world.

P OK. So can you tell us about some of the challenges that this expansion of population in London brought?

M Well, aside from the challenge of getting people from their homes to their jobs, perhaps the most obvious was the poverty. The streets were filled with beggars. Often whole families had to work long hours in factories in dreadful conditions. And of course disease was still an enormous problem in Victorian times. Cholera was endemic due to the unsanitary conditions in the city. There was no sewerage system. People used the river, which had become very polluted. In fact, the summer of 1858 is known as 'The Great Stink'.

P The Great Stink?

M Yes, because the city smelled so awful – so awful in fact that Parliament had to close down. In response to this, an engineer named Joseph Bazalgette was tasked with building a sewerage system for the city. He oversaw the construction of more than 1,100 miles of underground sewerage tunnels. Cholera disappeared from the city very soon after this and Bazalgette received a knighthood for his efforts.

P Interesting! So can I ask you to comment on 'parallels' between London and today's developing cities?

M Well, I think growing cities today face similar challenges. For example …

🔊 3.2

Well, today I'd like to talk about a very interesting urban development project – a new city called Masdar City. It's located in the desert not far from Abu Dhabi in the United Arab Emirates. It's interesting because it is going to be an eco-city – in fact the world's first zero-carbon city. To start, I'll explain the terms eco-city and zero-carbon. Then I'll give you some background to the project. After that I'll describe the city in some detail. Finally, I'll look at the feasibility of the project.

Let's begin with definitions. An eco-city is a city that is ecologically healthy – a city that takes account of the environment and makes as little impact on it as possible. This means that the inputs – of energy, water and food – are a minimum and the waste outputs – heat, air and water pollution are also as low as possible. A zero-carbon city goes further and reduces all emissions to nothing – to zero. So for example, transport in such a city would produce no pollution at all.

Let's turn to Masdar City itself. It's being built in the desert about 40 kilometres from Abu Dhabi, the UAE's capital city. It will eventually have a population of about 50,000 and there will be at least one thousand businesses and a university. The city is being designed by Foster and Partners, the famous British architecture firm. The total cost of the project will be between £10 and £20 billion, so it is not exactly cheap.

🔊 3.3

Now what about energy? We've already seen that eco-cities or zero-carbon cities use renewable energy sources – for example, wind power.

Well, in the UAE – one of the world's largest producers of fossil fuels, but also one of the hottest and driest countries in the world – they have decided to use the sun as a source of renewable energy, which seems an intelligent and far-sighted attitude. They have built the biggest solar farm in the Middle East to power the city. They are also experimenting with different ideas for generating power – for example using mirrors to concentrate light and thereby producing heat to drive generators.

Next I'd like to look at the cooling of the city. In the desert, of course, daytime temperatures are very high, more than 45 degrees in the summer, so how can a city of 50,000 people and 1,000 businesses be cooled efficiently?

Interestingly, Masdar City will use a variety of centuries-old strategies to keep the city comfortable. One method is the design of the city itself. Traditional Arab cities are very compact – the buildings are close together providing plenty of shade and helping keep cities cool.

Secondly, the walls will be covered with a special material, a terracotta mesh. This is a building material with holes in it. This material will keep the sun out but let the wind in and so will help keep the temperature down.

A third solution proposed is wind towers. These are traditional Arab buildings – tall, square towers with open sides at the top – they will catch any wind and direct it down into the streets and buildings.

Now let's move to another important area of 21st century life – What about transport? How will the inhabitants of Masdar City move about the city?

Well, firstly, it's very compact so people will be able to walk to most places. Streets will be pedestrianized – traffic-free. There will however be some transport – there will be special 'podcars'. These are driverless vehicles powered by solar energy. They stop and start automatically and are programmed to go where you ask. I rather like the sound of these podcars.

So finally what about the future? Well, the city is due to be completed around 2020 to 2025. In addition to helping the environment by being carbon-zero – the designers claim it will be a happy and healthy place for the inhabitants to live in. The air will be clean and pollution will be minimal.

🔊 3.4

Well, today I'd like to talk about a very interesting urban development project – a new city called Masdar City.

Let's begin with definitions. An eco-city is a city that is ecologically healthy …

Let's turn to Masdar City itself. It's being built in the desert about 40 kilometres from Abu Dhabi, the UAE's capital city.

Now what about energy? We've already seen that eco-cities or zero-carbon cities use renewable energy sources – for example, wind power.

Next I'd like to look at the cooling of the city. In the desert, of course, daytime temperature are very high, more than 45 degrees in the summer, so how can a city of 50,000 people and one thousand businesses be cooled efficiently?

Interestingly, Masdar City will use a variety of centuries-old strategies to keep the city comfortable. One method is the design of the city itself. Traditional Arab cities are very compact – the buildings are close together providing plenty of shade and helping keep cities cool.

Secondly, the walls will be covered with a special material, a terracotta mesh. This is a building material with holes in it. This material will keep the sun out but let the wind in and so will help to keep the temperature down.

A third solution proposed is wind towers. These are traditional Arab buildings – tall square towers with open sides at the top – they will catch any wind or slight breeze and direct it down into the streets and buildings.

Now let's move to another important area of 21st century life – what about transport? How will the inhabitants of Masdar City move about the city?

So finally, what about the future? Well, the city is due to be completed around 2020 to 2025.

 3.5

C = Carlos   S = Suzi   P = Peter

C What do you think about climate, Suzi?

S Well, Carlos, I think it's quite important but not as important as some of the other factors – for example, transport. It seems to me that all the best cities have good transport systems.

C Transport's not so important for me. Climate and culture and recreation – now these really are important. These should go at the top of the list.

S They are important but as I see it the most important thing is personal safety. You can have a nice climate and a lot of good recreational facilities but I think if you are worried about your personal safety then you can't enjoy living in a city. I really think we should put personal safety at the top of the list. What do you think, Peter?

P Well, as I see it all cities are dangerous to some extent, Suzi. You probably have to accept that wherever you live. So I agree with Carlos, I don't think personal safety should be high up the list. Perhaps we should put transport first and then climate second. Right, Carlos?

C Climate is very important. Who wants to live in a cold city where it rains all the year? Now Miami – that's a great place …

3.6

First, I'd like to talk about the climate of Dubai. Dubai can be uncomfortable during the summer months of June, July and August when the temperature rises to over 40 degrees, as you can see from this chart. But from October to April the weather is much cooler and then in the winter months – in December, January and February – the temperatures are very pleasant, below 30° by day and quite cool in the evening. Dubai has a dry climate, but there is some rain. The rainfall occurs mainly in the winter months as this second chart shows. February is the wettest month, but there is only 25mm of rain on average.

Now let's turn to the question of transport. Dubai has got many new roads, buses and most importantly a new, efficient and air-conditioned metro. All of this means that it's easy to get around Dubai and transport is affordable as well …

3.7

The population of many urban centres has increased dramatically in recent years. In fact, currently, over half of the world's population lives in cities. And another trend is the global increase in car ownership. There are now over 600 million cars in the world, which is almost one car for every ten people. It's when we put these two trends together that we start to see a real problem. Of course I'm referring to the amount of car traffic in cities around the world today. So, beyond the obvious annoyance of having to wait in queues, let's look at some of the other problems related to our overcrowded roads.

Pollution is one of the biggest resulting problems. Toxic fumes from automobiles have a negative impact on our health and on the air quality in our cities. This leads to rising healthcare and city maintenance costs. A study in the United States showed that traffic congestion annually costs the economy up to $1,000 per driver. Part of this is because people's time is wasted when they are stuck in traffic. They are often late for work and their time is not used in a productive way.

So what can be done about the problem of traffic congestion in cities? Well, urban planners have tried a variety of strategies. In London, for example, drivers pay a charge to use the roads in the city centre. A lot of people think this is a rather extreme solution but some cities are looking for an even more advanced approach. Urban planners in places such as Nagoya, in Japan, are trying to redesign the cities so that they can function without the use of any private cars at all.

3.8

Today I'm going to quickly talk about the city of London and some of the improvements which are being made to the city. First of all, I'll discuss transport and how the public transport system is being upgraded. Then I'd like to look at public spaces in London.

So I'd like to begin with transport. As some of you might know, London has the oldest underground system in the world. However, this means that some of the tunnels are small and the trains are very old-fashioned. They lack air conditioning and can frequently break down. But the city plans to improve several aspects of the underground system over the next ten years. Current train carriages will be replaced with more spacious and comfortable ones. Stations will be modernized, as some of these haven't seen upgrades in over 40 years.

Now let's move on to public spaces in London. The city is very fortunate in that it has some of the finest parks in any city in the world. This was a result of the fact that the parks belonged to the monarch – the king or queen – so building on the parks was never allowed. Currently, parks throughout London are seeing improvements, especially in areas such as cycle paths and modern, safer playgrounds for children. A separate project is focusing attention on places of historical significance within parks, and providing information for visitors.

4.1

P = Presenter   S = Sam   M = Mariam   L = Lee

P Hello and welcome to Global View – our weekly look at what is happening around the world. Today our topic is the global food crisis. What has caused this crisis – and what solutions can we find? Here with me in the studio is our panel of economists and journalists. First I'd like to introduce Sam Robinson, a journalist with the New York Telegraph.

S Hi.

P And next, Mariam Mangoli, an economist working for an African bank.

M Good evening.

P And finally, Lee Jin, a specialist on food production in the developing world.

L Hello.

P Well, let's start with you, Sam. What are the causes of the present food crisis throughout the world?

S I think there are a number of causes. One is the low productivity of farmers in the poorest countries in the world. It's not their fault really. They can't afford seeds, and fertilizers – and they can't pay for the water they need for irrigation.

P Miriam, what other factors are there?

M I agree with Sam. Low productivity is a problem, especially in Africa. But there are also what I would call natural causes. One is climate change. The recent droughts in Australia and Europe cut the global production of grain and this has contributed to the problem.

P Lee, I'd like to bring you in here. What do you see as the causes of this crisis?

L Another factor is population growth. In your introduction you called it a global food crisis, but there is also a global population crisis which has had an impact on food prices. There are clearly more mouths to feed, and together with rising incomes, there is a greater demand for food globally. Again we could call this a factor, like climate change, that we don't have a lot of control over. But there is one other cause of the crisis, which is clearly due to man's activities, and that is the production of biofuels.

S Can I come in here? I agree with Lee – biofuels have been a disaster. Governments in recent years have encouraged farmers to produce crops for fuel instead of crops for food. This has had a huge impact on food production.

P OK. Well, we seem to agree that there are four main causes of the present food crisis – low productivity, climate change, population growth, and also biofuels. But I'd like to move on now to consider solutions.

4.2

P = Presenter   S = Sam   M = Mariam   L = Lee

P What can we do? What practical steps can we take to solve this problem – this food crisis? Mariam?

M I'd like to come back to what I said earlier about climate change and drought. One thing we could do is to look at ways of making the world's crops 'weather-proof'. We could take steps to ensure that crops don't suffer during droughts. For example, in Africa – a simple thing like a farm pond. In the wet season the pond would collect water and this would be available in a drought.

P That seems like a very effective and very simple solution. Lee?

L I mentioned earlier the problem with biofuels, so I think another simple solution would be to stop this investment in biofuels. Let farmers produce food again – not fuel. It is food that the world needs from them. As far as fuel is concerned, governments have to find alternatives to solve this crisis – but not biofuels.

P OK. But let's go back to the first point we made – about low productivity. Sam – what can we do about this central issue? Are there any easy ways to increase productivity?

S Yes, there are. As I said at the beginning of our discussion, just give the farmers seeds, fertilizers and water – that's what they need. Now some people will say that this is a very expensive solution. But in fact it is not as expensive as the alternative for these countries, which is importing food. Let's look at the example of Malawi. Agriculture was very unproductive. Malawi had to import basic food – like maize! So what did the government do? They gave farmers subsidized seeds – high yield seeds – and subsidized fertilizers. Within two years Malawi was exporting maize, not importing it.

P So maybe Malawi is a model for other countries.

4.3

Hello. My name's Joshua Toure. I'm from the African Agricultural Agency based in Nairobi. As you all know there is a global food crisis caused by a number of factors which have all come together at the same time. But what I want to do today is to show you how we can tackle this crisis by using small-scale projects – small, local initiatives which are supported by international aid agencies. My examples today all come from the southern African state of Malawi.

4.4

Let me begin by showing you the location of Malawi. It's here in south-eastern Africa. It lies along the shores of Lake Malawi and is bordered by Zambia, Mozambique and Tanzania.

And here on this slide are a few facts and figures about the country. The capital city is Lilongwe – that's L-I-L-O-N-G-W-E. It's a rapidly growing city – the population is now nearly 1 million. Not so long ago it was just a small village on the banks of a river. The population

of the country as a whole is just over 12 million. But it is not a very large country in area – about 118,000 sq km. It's about the same size as Cuba or North Korea. The life expectancy of its population is 36 – yes that's right just 36 years – due mainly to the high incidence of disease in the country.

Now if we look at the climate chart for Malawi we can see that there are two distinct seasons in the year: the rainy season, which lasts from December to May; and the dry season from June to November. In some years when rainfall is lower than average, farmers face great difficulties.

Malawi is an agricultural country. Tobacco is its most valuable export. But its main staple crop, that is, the crop that provides food for its people, is maize – corn. So maize has a very important role in the economy.

4.5 [including 4.6]

Now what are the problems facing farmers? Here you can see the three main problems: lack of regular water supplies, poor soil quality and thirdly yields – that is the amount of produce farmers get from their land – yields are low.

First, the problem of water. This slide shows a family working in their field. The crop in the field is maize. In the past the family was only able to produce one harvest a year, during the rainy season. But a new irrigation project, using water from a stream to irrigate the fields of eight villages in the region, has transformed their lives. This family are now able to harvest up to three times a year.

And here you can see the channel that was built to bring water to their fields. It has really transformed the lives of this family and other people living in the area! Now they can grow crops in the dry season.

Another way that food production has been increased in Malawi is by the distribution of subsidized high yield seeds and legumes – that's plants like beans, peas, lentils, and so on. The seeds and legumes are sold to farmers at low prices. Similarly, the government distributes subsidized fertilizers.

[4.6 starts] What are the results of these initiatives to help farmers? Quite dramatic, as you can see from the graph. Corn production in Malawi had fallen sharply from a high point in 2000 of around 2.5 million metric tonnes down to around 1.5 million in 2002 and 2003. In 2005, the year this policy was introduced, the total was just 1.7 million metric tonnes, still well below the 2000 level. However, the following year, 2006, production jumped dramatically to 2.7 million metric tonnes, and again in 2007, to 3.4 million metric tonnes. A 27% increase from the previous year – a remarkable achievement.

So, what does all this show? Is Malawi a model for the rest of Africa? I think it is. Small-scale projects are the answer – projects designed to give farmers what they need. And the three things they need most are – first, seeds, that is, high yield seeds – second, fertilizers – and thirdly, of course, a regular supply of water.

To conclude the global food crisis can be solved if we adopt this slogan – Think Globally–Act Locally. As I said at the beginning it is a global crisis but it needs to be tackled by small projects that take into account the knowledge and the needs of local people and if we can do that then … [4.6 ends]

4.7

Today I want to talk about biofuels. There are two main types – ethanol and biodiesel. Ethanol can be used in ordinary cars. It comes from crops, plants such as sugar cane and grains. Biodiesel on the other hand comes from plants such as oil palm and soybean. The countries which use biofuels the most include Brazil, the USA, and France. Biofuels are generally used for transport – for cars, lorries, buses and planes.

Now what about the process of making biofuels? Take ethanol as an example. Well, firstly the plants are grown like normal crops. When they are ready they are collected – harvested – and then transported to a refinery – a bio-refinery – where the plants are converted by chemical processes into ethanol. This is then distributed to petrol stations and sold as biofuel to motorists …

🔊 4.8

S = Samira   M = Mike   H = Hiroto

S Who would like to start the discussion? Mike?

M Well, it seems to me that the introduction of biofuels has been a mistake. I can see why this was done but these crops take up a lot of valuable agricultural land that could be used for producing food. And what's more because the land is being used for biofuel crops it pushes up food prices. Hiroto, what do you think?

H I agree. Rising food prices are a real problem, especially for the poorer regions of the world. We have seen food riots as people have protested about rising food prices. But in the long term, I can't see any other alternative. We know that oil, gas, and coal will run out one day. We have to explore other sources. Samira, what do you think?

S What about solar power, wind power, and other renewable sources?

H These have a part to play but so far they make up just a small percentage of our needs. I think biofuel is easily produced and probably a lot cheaper than other renewable sources, solar energy for example. Samira?

S Well I agree that biofuels are easily produced. And also they can be grown locally. There is no need to transport the fuel halfway around the world like we have to with oil, for example. So there are a lot of positive points, but on the other hand I do feel they are pushing up the price of food and this is a very important concern. And we have to think about the effect these crops may have on the soil. It's really quite a difficult choice …

🔊 4.9

1 109,773   2 15,675,000   3 36%   4 78.95   5 0.245   6 ¾

🔊 4.10

Hello. Today I'm going to talk briefly about my country, Tunisia. I'll start off by giving you some facts and figures about the country before going on to talk about agriculture in detail. Now I expect you all know where Tunisia is. It's in North Africa, located between Algeria in the west and Libya in the east. It borders the Mediterranean Sea. The area of the country is not very large, 163,610 sq km. I'll repeat that if you didn't catch it – 163,610 sq km. So it is larger than Greece, for example, but a lot smaller than Libya, our neighbour to the east. The population of the country taken from the 2006 estimate is just over 10 million, 10,175,014 to be exact – that's 10,175,014, but I am sure it has increased since then.

The climate of Tunisia varies from the north to the south. In the north we have mild rainy winters and hot dry summers – so it is a typical Mediterranean climate. The south, however, is a desert region and it is hot and dry all year. Life expectancy is high in Tunisia – 75.12 years. Some people say this is because of our healthy diet. Finally, in this introduction, I'd like to mention the main crops – these are firstly, wheat, then tomatoes, and lastly olives. Last year, wheat production in metric tonnes was 1,360,000 – tomatoes – 920,000 and thirdly olives – 700,000 metric tonnes.

Now I'd like to move on to a more detailed description of agriculture in Tunisia …

🔊 4.11

One point one billion people throughout the world don't have sufficient access to safe, clean drinking water. This is referred to as the 'water crisis'. Experts have identified several causes for the water crisis. One cause is deforestation. You see, trees hold water in the ground. When an area of trees is cut down to make room for farms or urban development, this reduces the amount of underground water. This is especially noticeable in tropical rainforests, which produce about 30% of our planet's fresh water. Unfortunately, many tropical rainforests are undergoing serious deforestation. So what can be done to solve this problem? Well, reforestation has been taking place on a small scale in some regions, but before that, I think education is the real answer. Citizens and governments need to be educated in how deforestation can lead to very serious problems. Only after there is a broad understanding of the risks, can we begin to undo some of the damage which has already been caused.

🔊 5.1

J = Jane   L = Lee   S = Sunil   M = Miriam

J I think we need to discuss two questions. Firstly, to what extent is the globalization of culture actually happening? Lee, how do you see it?

L Well, Jane, personally, I think we have to be careful here not to exaggerate the globalization of culture. I think it is a good thing, but it may not be as widespread as the media seem to think. There are still many areas of the world that have kept their own culture. China, for example. What do the rest of you think? Miriam?

M I think it is happening – the cultural boundaries the author mentions in the article – these boundaries have gone. I see it all around – fashion, for example.

S Yes, all these designer clothes – Adidas, Versace, Jimmy Choo – you see them everywhere.

M And it is the same with entertainment. I read recently that *House* is the most popular TV programme in the world – it is watched in more than 60 countries – 60!

J What about food? I think there are certain foods that are popular all over the world. I think that is a sign of globalization too. What do you think, Sunil?

S Certainly. Take pizza for example – pizza was once only an Italian snack – and now you find it in almost every country you go to. I read recently that Pizza Hut has 34,000 restaurants in 100 different countries. And I think the result of that can be the suppression of local culture. Lee, what's your view on this?

L Well, as I said earlier, I think there is some globalization of culture, but I think local culture is still strong. I visited Moscow recently – and yes, it's true that there are McDonalds and Pizza Hut and so on – but at home people eat Russian food. That hasn't changed. Miriam?

M Well, Jane, I think most of us seem to be in agreement on this question. There is a trend towards the globalization of culture.

J So, what about the second question – is this move towards a global culture (if it is happening) a good thing? Or does it mean that local cultures will disappear? Would anyone like to comment?

M Well, to me it seems we all end up the same – doing the same thing and eating the same food. On the whole, I am against this trend. Sunil?

S Well, I look at it this way – globalization of culture brings people together – you will have a shared culture. This means that wherever you go in the world you will feel at home. There will be people who speak English, you will recognize the restaurants and coffee shops, you can use the Internet and your mobile phone. And when you meet people in these countries you will have things in common – things to talk about – the World Cup, for example, or cricket or the Olympics.

L Yes. And you can see the same films and satellite TV programmes – and also buy the clothes you like to buy in your home country. My brother is in China and he saw the film *Avatar* there. He saw it before I did!

M I think we are getting away from the issue here. If I go to another country I like to see something new – a different culture – different food, different things to buy in the shops – a different way of life. I don't want everything I can get at home!

J So what you are saying is that globalization makes travel less interesting.

M Exactly. We are all going to be the same so there will be nothing new to learn.

J I think I agree with Miriam on this. The world will become less interesting. Sunil, what's your view on this?

S Well, I'm afraid I don't agree. There will still be a lot to learn – and you will have a choice. If you want to try local food, you can – but if you are in a hurry or you are not adventurous you can have the food you know.

M And another thing – what about language? That's part of culture too. If everybody speaks English, local languages will suffer. Some may disappear.

L That's true. A lot of smaller languages are already disappearing.

M And local customs and local values – all of that will go – replaced by Western values.

S No, that's not true, Miriam. We will still have our local values – the things we learn from our parents – but in addition we will have common international or global values. I think that's great. After all, we are all living on the same planet!

J Well, I agree with Sunil we are all living on the same planet and things that bring us closer together are good. On the other hand I think Miriam has a point. It is a pity to see local culture destroyed.

L No! Local cultures are not destroyed. They are – what's the word in the article? – supplemented by another culture – an additional culture – which is global culture.

J We seem to be divided on this. Let me just summarize what we've been saying in this discussion. I think we all agree that globalization of culture is happening to some extent – but not all of us think it is a good thing. Those in favour say that it is a good thing because it means that we will have …

 5.2

J = Jane   L = Lee   S = Sunil   M = Miriam

J So, what about the second question – is this move towards a global culture (if it is happening) a good thing? Or does it mean that local cultures will disappear? Would anyone like to comment?

M Well, to me it seems we all end up the same – doing the same thing and eating the same food. On the whole, I am against this trend. Sunil?

S Well, I look at it this way – globalization of culture brings people together – you will have a shared culture. This means that wherever you go in the world you will feel at home. There will be people who speak English, you will recognize the restaurants and coffee shops, you can use the Internet and your mobile phone. And when you meet people in these countries you will have things in common – things to talk about – the World Cup, for example, or cricket or the Olympics.

L Yes. And you can see the same films and satellite TV programmes – and also buy the clothes you like to buy in your home country. My brother is in China and he saw the film *Avatar* there. He saw it before I did!

M I think we are getting away from the issue here. If I go to another country I like to see something new – a different culture – different food, different things to buy in the shops – a different way of life. I don't want everything I can get at home!

J So what you are saying is that globalization makes travel less interesting.

M Exactly. We are all going to be the same so there will be nothing new to learn.

J I think I agree with Miriam on this. The world will become less interesting. Sunil, what's your view on this?

S Well, I'm afraid I don't agree. There will still be a lot to learn – and you will have a choice. If you want to try local food, you can – but if you are in a hurry or you are not adventurous you can have the food you know.

 5.3

J = Jane   L = Lee   S = Sunil   M = Miriam

S Yes, – all these designer labels clothes – Adidas, Versace, Jimmy Choo – you see them everywhere.

M And it is the same with entertainment. I read recently that *House* is the most popular TV programme in the world – it is watched in more than 60 countries – 60!

S I read recently that Pizza Hut has 34,000 restaurants in 100 different countries.

L Well, as I said earlier. I think there is some globalization of culture, but I think local culture is still strong. I visited Moscow recently – and yes it's true that there are McDonalds and Pizza Hut and so on – but at home people eat Russian food. That hasn't changed.

J Yes. And you can see the same films and satellite TV programmes – and also buy the clothes you like to buy in your home country. My brother is in China and he saw the film *Avatar* there. He saw it before I did!

 5.4 [including 5.5, 5.6, 5.7]

[5.5 starts] We've been discussing globalization recently and the cultural aspects of this phenomenon – the fact that as globalization develops all parts of the world seem to be getting closer and closer to one another culturally. Perhaps you remember the term I used last time – Global Village.

Well, today I want to talk about one example of global culture – and in particular one internationally famous company – Starbucks. I'll start off with a brief history of Starbucks – a timeline from its origins in 1971 – and then I'll look at the current situation – the extent of the Starbucks chain across the world – and finally, I'll discuss the implications of this expansion. [5.5 ends]

[5.6 starts] Starbucks was founded in 1971 by three friends in Seattle in the US. At first, they just sold coffee beans and coffee-making equipment. In 1982, a business entrepreneur Howard Schultz – that's Howard – H-O-W-A-R-D – Schultz – S-C-H-U-L-T-Z – joined the company as Marketing Director. Schultz went to Italy and while there he was very impressed with Italian coffee bars. He came back and tried to persuade the company to open coffee bars, serving Italian-style coffee. His idea wasn't accepted so he left the company and in 1986 started his own chain of coffee bars, which became very successful. The following year – 1987 – Schultz bought the Starbucks chain. Expansion continued and Starbucks started to open coffee bars outside Seattle – in fact, all across North America. 1996 was another important date in the history of Starbucks. This was when the first Starbucks was opened outside North America. It was in Tokyo, Japan. And in 1998 they entered the UK market – buying up a chain of UK-owned coffee shops. From there Starbucks expanded rapidly across the globe. By 2003, they had more than 6,400 outlets worldwide. Between 2001 and 2004, they opened 1,200 new stores every year – that's 1,200 new stores every year. Imagine that! [5.6 ends]

[5.7 starts] So what is the situation today? Has this expansion continued? Well, currently there are over 16,000 Starbucks in more than 50 countries worldwide from Argentina, to the UAE, to China. 50 countries! So it really is a global brand. Starbucks have plans for as many as 30,000 stores across the world – 30,000, with China becoming second only to the US in the number of outlets.

Nowadays, Starbucks is not just a coffee shop. They serve coffee of course, but they also serve snacks and soft drinks. They offer free WiFi access in their stores, so coffee drinkers can browse the Internet on their laptops while enjoying a cappuccino.

What kind of company is Starbucks? Starbucks prides itself on being a responsible business. For example, the coffee they buy is Fair Trade certified and all the cups they use are either recycled or reusable.

Finally, in this brief overview of Starbucks, I'd like to look at the implications of the rise of Starbucks and similar companies.

What does it all mean? Well, Starbucks is an example of a truly global company. Let me quote from their website: *'Our stores are a welcoming place for meeting friends and family, enjoying a quiet moment alone with a book, or simply finding a familiar place in a new city.'* That last point is important. Starbucks offers customers *'a familiar place in a new city'.*

Opponents of globalization say that companies like Starbucks are bad for local businesses. They argue local coffee shops will go out of business because they cannot compete with a global giant. They also claim that they are limiting choice – all coffee shops will eventually become the same. On the other hand there are those who say that companies like Starbucks are simply giving people what they want – comfortable coffee shops where they can meet friends, enjoy coffee and use their laptops. Because it's a global brand, they know wherever they are in the world they can get the same product and the same standard of service.

In conclusion, we have to say – even if some people don't like the idea of a global culture as represented by companies like Starbucks, it's a fact of life. The world really is becoming a global village. [5.7 ends]

🔊 5.8

A = Andy   B = Beth

A Hello. I'm from Manchester University. We're conducting a survey on street markets. Could I ask you a few questions?

B Yes, certainly.

A Thank you. First of all, do you live in Manchester?

B Yes, I do. I live in Didsbury.

A Now, how often do you shop in this market – daily, three or four times a week, once a week, monthly, or less often.

B Less often – probably about once a month.

A Right. And why do you like shopping here?

B Well, the products are nice and fresh – and the prices are good too. They're often cheaper than in the supermarkets.

A OK. Now how important is price for you when you are shopping? Can you say on a scale of 5 to 1 – where 5 is very important.

B Hmmm – you say 5 is very important? Well, in that case 4.

A Now, how do you get to the market? Walking, by bus, by car or other.

B I have to get a bus here. It takes about 20 minutes.

A I see. And can I ask about the type of products you buy? What do you usually buy here?

B Well, I like the fish. I think it's fresh. And I buy fruit as well. And there's a nice stall where they sell bread. I usually buy some bread.

🔊 5.9

Now let's turn to the results of the survey. You can see from this pie chart that almost all of the shoppers we spoke to – our survey sample – came from Manchester – nearly 90%. Only a few came from outside the city.

The second chart shows how often the shoppers came to the market. You can see that the majority of our sample shop in the market on a weekly basis – around 55%. Surprisingly, quite a few shop there on a daily basis – just about 20%. And 15% come three or four times a week. The others came monthly or less often.

Next we asked the shoppers how important price was for them on a scale of 5 – very important – down to 1. As you can see from the bar chart most people chose 5 or 4 – about 50% said 5 – very important – and 35% said 4 – important. Just 15% chose 3 and interestingly no one chose 2 or 1.

Then we wanted to find out how people came to the market. We gathered this data on Wednesday and on Saturday to see if there is any difference. The table shows quite clearly that the majority of shoppers, just over 55%, walked to the market on Wednesday. We think this might be because they work in the area. On Saturday, that figure was lower, around 35%, as people were less likely to walk to

the market from their homes. About 30% said they came by bus on a weekday, while at the weekend it was noticeably higher. Only a few came by car – about 10% on both days. The rest of the people came by other means of transport – by bicycle or taxi.

We asked people why they liked shopping in the market. We had a number of different answers but the main points that came up were that the produce was cheap and also fresh …

🔊 5.10

M = May   A = Alberto   R = Rita

M So, we've discussed how technology has lead to the globalization of culture, but could there be other factors as well? What do you think, Alberto?

A Well, I don't know, May. I think technology obviously has a role in it, but so do migration and travel. People are moving around a lot more than they used to. The reason there are Vietnamese restaurants in London is because people from Vietnam moved to London, not because people living in London read about Vietnamese food on the Internet …

M Well …

A Would you like to comment on that, May?

M Yes, thanks. I see what you're saying, but it's a matter of scale. The huge increase in globalized culture is very recent. Populations have been moving around for ages, but only in the last – what, thirty years? twenty years? – have we seen this kind of uniform culture across the globe. As a result of this, I think technology has to be considered the most important cause. Rita, what's your view?

R You both make good points, but I don't think we should leave out market factors.

A I'm not sure if I'm following you, Rita, could you explain that.

R Globalized culture has been spread by big companies looking for new markets to sell their products into. Look at Starbucks. They are a big international company who want to find new places to sell their coffee. Every time they open a branch in a new place, the globalization of culture spreads that much further.

🔊 5.11

Another international company that I imagine you've heard of, or been to, is the Swedish furniture company, IKEA. So IKEA was started by Ingvar Kamprad – that's I-N-G-V-A-R – K-A-M-P-R-A-D. It was founded in 1943 and the first IKEA store was opened in Almhult. I'll spell that too, it's A-L-M-H-U-L-T, in Sweden, in the year 1958. By 1963, there was an IKEA store in Norway. It spread rapidly throughout the 1970s and 80s and now – you'll want to note this down – there are over 250 stores in over 40 countries.

🔊 6.1 [including 6.2, 6.3]

P = Presenter   T = Tomas Olearski

[6.2 starts] **P** Hello and welcome to World Report. With me in the studio today is Dr Tomas Olearski – an architect and historian who has worked closely with World Heritage for many years. Tomas, let me start by asking you about World Heritage. What exactly is it? And when did it begin?

T Well, the initial idea for the World Heritage Programme came about in 1954. The Egyptian government were planning the construction of the Aswan High Dam on the River Nile. This project, which would help to control the seasonal flooding of the river and generate electricity, unfortunately endangered the Abu Simbel and Philae Temple complexes.

P So these temples would have been flooded by the reservoir created by this dam?

T That's right. They would have been lost forever. This came to the attention of the United Nations, and it was decided that the temples had to be saved. The rationale was that these monuments were humanity's heritage, rather than one nation's, and we all share responsibility to protect our common heritage.

P So, what happened to the temples?

T They were physically moved to a new site – higher land – away from the dam. More than $80 million was provided by countries contributing to the United Nations. These temples are unique – to let them be covered by flood-water would have been a great loss for all of mankind. The World Heritage Programme grew out of the success of this project and finally in 1972 the convention – the World Heritage Convention – was ratified. That is to say, the nations in the UN agreed on a text outlining the goals of the programme.

P Could you briefly explain what some of these goals are?

T The basic goal of the UNESCO World Heritage Programme is to help preserve heritage sites – to keep them for future generations. This goal is achieved by a number of steps. First the organization provides money and resources to maintain sites which are in immediate danger – sites such as Abu Simbel. It also helps with the day-to-day maintenance of heritage sites by providing technical assistance and training programmes. And thirdly, it helps to raise public awareness of these sites. The publicity generated for sites on the World Heritage list can result in a substantial increase in tourist revenues.

P It sounds as though it is very beneficial for countries participating in this programme. About how many countries are part of this scheme?

T The number has increased over the years. To date, 187 have ratified the convention.

P So 187 have agreed to the aims of the convention?

T That's right. [6.2 ends]

[6.3 starts] **P** Now, can you tell me why, in your opinion, we need an international organization for this? Can't countries look after their own heritage – their own important sites?

T A good question. But the fact is that many countries – for whatever reason – do not, or cannot, protect their cultural or natural sites. There may be wars in that region, or maybe the government does not consider it an important issue, or more likely they simply do not have the resources to protect these sites. Also we believe that these wonderful places – the mountain railways of India, or the Jurassic coast of Dorset in the UK, for example, belong to all of us – are a part of the world's heritage. It is our duty to protect these places for future generations.

P Now, I believe there are about 900 World Heritage sites all over the world …

T Yes. 911 at the moment. The number is increasing all the time.

P And how many of these 911 are cultural sites?

T There are 704 cultural sites and 180 natural sites. And there are also 27 sites which we say are 'mixed'. They are of both cultural and natural importance.

P Where are these heritage sites? Are they mainly in Europe and America?

T No, no. They are all over the world – Asia, Africa, South America – in 151 different states to be exact. Let me explain what these sites are. The cultural sites may include buildings such as the Sydney Opera House – or monuments such as the Abu Simbel Temples, or perhaps whole cities – like Verona in Italy. Cultural sites also include places which have special significance for mankind – for example the Hiroshima Peace Memorial in Japan. The natural sites, on the other hand, include forests, mountains, lakes, deserts and so on. So for example, the tropical rainforest of Sumatra in Indonesia is a World Heritage Site, Mount Kenya in Africa, and Lake Baikal in Russia. An example of a mixed site would be Cappadocia in Turkey where there are unique features of geology and also unique settlements – houses built into rocks.

P How do you select these sites? How do you decide that this building or forest or desert is important, but another place is not?

T It is difficult. But we use ten criteria altogether. For example, a cultural site could show an important stage of human history – the development of early man, for example – or a natural site might be important for conserving a threatened species – the tiger for example. This is an important criterion.

P What is the procedure for getting a site recognized as a World Heritage Site? For example, if I think a certain building in my city should be on the list, what should I do?

T I'm afraid nomination starts with countries not individuals. So first a country should make a list of important cultural and historical sites which it thinks should be a World Heritage Site. We call this a Tentative List – a list of possible sites. Well, from that list of possibles the country then selects one site that it thinks is really important and adds it to a Nomination File. The file is inspected and the nominations are passed to the World Heritage Committee. The committee meets once a year and decides whether to add this site to the list of World Heritage Sites or not. [6.3 ends]

 6.4

I'm very pleased to welcome our speaker today, Rosie Sanders. Professor Sanders is a well-known archaeologist from the University of London. She's a specialist in the Middle East and has visited the region on many occasions. Today's illustrated talk is part of the series 'Saving the Past'. It is about Bahla Fort, which is located in the interior of Oman. This fort is now a UNESCO World Heritage Site. In this talk, Professor Sanders will describe the town of Bahla and then look at the history of the fort. Finally, she will describe the continuing restoration of the fort with the help of UNESCO and the Omani government.

6.5

Hello. Thank you for that kind welcome. Today I want to talk to you about a very interesting fort located in Oman. The name of the fort is Bahla and it is now a UNESCO World Heritage Site.

The oasis town of Bahla, set in the heart of Oman, is famous for many reasons. As you can see from this picture, Bahla is surrounded by date palm trees. The water in this dry, arid part of Oman comes from the nearby Jebel Akhdar or Green Mountain, which you can see in the distance, and for many centuries this has given life to Bahla. In the past, wheat, barley, cotton, and sugar cane were cultivated here, but today the main agricultural crop is dates.

The next picture shows you the view from the top of the fort. From here you can see how green the whole oasis is. In fact Bahla is really a collection of villages – some 46 villages set within the oasis – and surrounded by a long defensive wall.

This is the souk – the local market – which is really the centre of the town. Here the products from the farms are sold – vegetables, fruit, and of course, dates. There is also a livestock market – for goats, chickens, and so on. And here you can buy the famous Bahla pottery produced by Bahla's own potters.

But more important than the market or pottery is the fort. This picture shows a view of Bahla Fort taken from the souk area. Oman has a lot of forts spread all over the country but this is the oldest and largest fort in Oman.

The fort dates from around the 13th or 14th centuries when Bahla was an important trading centre and the home of the powerful Banu Nebhan tribe. It was very large – the walls are 12 kilometres in length – and the towers are more than 50 metres high. It was built of brick and sandstone – sandstone for the foundations and bricks made of mud for the walls. But over the years because of wars between tribes – and the effects of the sun and rain – the fort walls and towers deteriorated. By the 1980s the whole structure was in very poor condition – in fact a ruin. The towers had collapsed and the walls of the main buildings had fallen down too.

However, in 1987 Bahla fort became a UNESCO World Heritage Site and in 1988 was added to the list of World Heritage Sites in Danger, a list buildings or environments in immediate danger of being lost to the world. So the situation in Bahla was serious. But from this point on things began to improve for Bahla Fort.

In the 1990s work began on restoring the fort. Over $9 million was spent by the Omani government and for many years the structure was covered in scaffolding, as this slide shows. The building was closed to tourists while the reconstruction work was carried out. Eventually in 2004, the fort was removed from the World Heritage list of endangered buildings. The walls, the towers, and the fort itself have all been restored to what they used to be – using original building materials – mud and stone. Some parts had to be completely rebuilt. The reconstruction is nearly finished and the fort really does look as good as new.

Now Bahla Fort will soon be open again to visitors and I'm sure it will become a very popular tourist attraction. The fact that it is a World Heritage Site – one of only four in Oman – has given it a lot of publicity and its future should be secured.

So to summarize, I've told you a little about the oasis town of Bahla and its history, the story of its fort, and how it became a World Heritage Site and was eventually restored. In conclusion, I'd like to say that Bahla Fort represents a great example of what can be done, with effort and money, to preserve our heritage. These treasures from the past must be preserved for future generations to enjoy.

6.6

A We can see from this chart that Africa has 33 natural sites, 42 cultural sites, 3 mixed sites making a total of 78 sites. The Arab States, on the other hand, have 4 natural sites, 60 cultural sites and only 1 mixed site. The total number of sites is 65. Next we have the Asia-Pacific region. Here there are 48 natural sites, 129 cultural sites and 9 mixed sites, which makes a total of 186 sites. Now let's look at the Latin American and Caribbean region. The number of natural sites is 35. There are 83 cultural sites and 3 mixed sites. The total is 121. Finally, the totals for all of the regions. The total number of natural sites is …

B To begin with I'd like to explain how many sites there are and where they are located. This table shows World Heritage Sites by region and it also shows which are natural sites, which are cultural, and which are mixed – meaning they have both cultural and natural importance. As you can see there are 5 different regions: Africa, the Arab States, Asia-Pacific, Europe and the United States – as one region, and finally Latin America and the Caribbean. The total number of sites is shown here – 890. The majority – 689 – are cultural sites – and only a few are mixed sites. The region with the largest number of sites is Europe, United States and Canada – 440 – followed by Asia-Pacific with 186 sites. The region with the smallest number of sites is the Arab States – only 65. It is interesting to note here that only 4 of the sites in this region are of natural importance. Perhaps this is because in these dry, arid countries there is little flora or fauna to protect …

6.7

Speaker A Well, that's it really about the Everglades – it really is an interesting place. By the way, if you are in Florida you should go to Key West. It's not far from the Everglades – it's an island, but you can get there by road. There's a bridge that links all the islands until you get there. OK. Thanks for listening.

Speaker B I hope I have given you a clear picture of the problems faced by the Everglades. I described the location of the Everglades and how the region was formed. I also mentioned the wildlife that you can find there. Finally, I discussed the criteria that were used to select the Everglades as a World Heritage Site and why it has recently been placed on the 'in danger' list.

Speaker C To sum up, I've tried to show you that the Everglades is a unique natural environment. I mentioned the history of the region and how the marshes were formed. We also discussed the wide variety of flora and fauna to be found in the region. Lastly

I looked at the status of the Everglades as a World Heritage Site and how it has recently become classified as being 'in danger'. We need to wake up to what we are doing to the Everglades. If we don't act now we may lose this wonderful natural wilderness, and it will be lost forever. Thank you. Are there any questions?

6.8

M = Martin   A = Andrea Evans

M On the 'Your Community' podcast today we're talking to Andrea Evans, who is a member of the town's Preservation Committee.

A Hello, it's nice to be here, Martin.

M Could you explain what it is exactly that the Preservation Committee does?

A It's a five-person committee and we work hard to raise awareness about buildings of historical significance in our town. We also award funding to buildings or groups that want to take part in civic conservation. If the owner of an historic building needs financial help to preserve that building, they can apply to the committee for a grant.

M How much would a typical grant be?

A Well, anywhere up to £50,000 or so.

M And could you tell us the process you use to award this funding?

A The building owner submits a proposal, which includes why the building is historically significant – it has to satisfy certain criteria, you see – if it is an important example of an architectural style, or alternatively, if something significant happened in this place.

M Could you give us an example?

A For example, if an historically significant person lived there. So, if they satisfy some of the criteria, and show that they have a good plan in place for the future, we can begin to discuss how much is needed. But I should point out that we help in other ways as well. We provide educational support.

M What do you mean by that? Do you go into schools?

A No. That's a good idea, though. What I meant is that we provide information and resources to building owners and conservation groups – not only about maintenance and that sort of thing, but basic legal advice and strategic planning for the future. We help them inform the public about their particular site.

M And do you think that there is much public awareness of the historical buildings in our town?

A Well, no I don't actually, but that's starting to change.

7.1

An airport consists of at least one surface such as a runway for a plane to take off and land, and often includes buildings such as control towers, hangars and terminal buildings. An airport terminal is a building where passengers transfer between ground transportation and the facilities that allow them to board and disembark from aircraft. Within the terminal, passengers purchase tickets, transfer their luggage, and go through security. Terminals provide access to the aeroplanes via departure and arrival gates. Larger terminals have a range of facilities for passengers including restaurants, shops, and relaxation areas.

7.2

K = Kate   B = Bill

K In today's podcast we'll be looking at three of the largest and most famous airports in the world – in China, Spain and Singapore. In fact, one of them was recently voted the world's best airport. All three are stunning examples of modern airport design by some of the world's leading architectural firms. And we'll be looking at some of the design issues. How can you make sure that tens of thousands of people arrive and leave the airport efficiently? How can you make airport buildings that are sustainable – that use as little energy as possible? And equally importantly, how can you make sure that passengers have a comfortable and attractive environment to relax in before they depart?

Let's start with the first of the three. Here is Bill Thomas to tell us about a stunning new airport.

B This is Beijing Capital International Airport, currently the biggest airport in the world. It was finished in 2008, just in time for the 2008 Olympics. Designed by Foster and Partners, it has turned out to be a very efficient building in terms of operational efficiency and passenger comfort. It is also very sustainable in its design – for example, great use is made of natural light. The design of the airport reflects Chinese culture. From the air it looks like a flying dragon and inside the airport, the use of traditional Chinese colours – red and golden yellow – and the red columns stretching into the distance make you think of a Chinese temple. According to Norman Foster, the architect, this is a building born of its context. It will be a true gateway to the nation. The newly built Terminal 3 building and the Ground Transportation Centre together enclose a floor area of approximately 1.3 million square metres, mostly under one roof – the first building, by the way, to go over the 1 million square metre mark. Passenger numbers at the airport are currently around 42 million passengers per annum so it is also one of the world's busiest.

K Now let's move from Asia to Europe and to Barajas Airport in Madrid, Bill.

B Barajas Airport is the main international airport serving Madrid in Spain. The country's largest and busiest airport is the world's 11th busiest airport with around 29 million passengers a year. The airport name derives from the adjacent district of Barajas, which has its own metro station on the same rail line serving the airport. The main part of the airport, Terminal 4, was designed by Richard Rogers, and it was inaugurated on February 5, 2006. Rogers is a world famous architect known for the use of steel and glass in his buildings. Terminal 4 in Barajas is one of the world's largest airport terminals in terms of area, at 760,000 square metres. The building is meant to give passengers a stress-free start to their journey. This is managed through careful use of illumination, available by using glass panes instead of walls and numerous domes in the roof, which allow natural light to pass through. The roof consists of a series of waves formed by huge wings of prefabricated steel. Internally, the roof is covered in bamboo strips, giving it a smooth and seamless appearance. In contrast, structural trees are painted to create a kilometre-long vista of graduated colour – a fabulous and colourful effect.

K Finally, let's go back to Asia and look at another modern airport which has recently been voted the best airport in the world.

B Changi Airport in Singapore was named the best airport in the world according to a recent survey. The airport's new Terminal 3 finally commenced operations in January 2008 after years of anticipation and a cost of $1.75 billion. It was designed by the architectural and engineering firm, CPG Consultants. Terminal 3's most outstanding feature is a unique 'butterfly' roof which allows soft natural light into the building while keeping the tropical heat out. The one-of-its-kind roof design has 919 skylights with specially-designed reflector panels which adjust automatically to allow an optimal amount of soft and uniform daylight into the terminal building. Another key highlight of Terminal 3 is a five-storey high vertical garden called 'The Green Wall'. Spanning 300 metres across the main building, it can be admired from the departure and arrival halls, and baggage carousels. The Green Wall is covered with climbing plants and is interspersed with four cascading waterfalls.

The area of the building is 430,000 square metres. Terminal 3 adds a capacity of 22 million passengers per annum to Changi Airport, bringing the airport's total annual capacity to about 70 million passengers.

7.3

1 This is Beijing Capital International Airport, currently the biggest airport in the world.

2 It was finished in 2008 just in time for the 2008 Olympics. Designed by Foster and Partners, it turned out to be a very efficient building in terms of operational efficiency and passenger comfort.

3 The design of the airport reflects Chinese culture. From the air it looks like a flying dragon and inside the airport the use of traditional Chinese colours – red and golden yellow – and the red columns stretching into the distance make you think of a Chinese temple.

7.4

Today I want to talk about green architecture and specifically about green skyscrapers. We'll be looking at two buildings in particular which are regarded as fine examples of green buildings. One is in China – the Pearl River Tower and the second is the Bank of America building in New York – two of the best examples of green buildings in the world. I'll be describing the buildings and then looking at their special 'green' features. But before that I want to look at the concept of green architecture in general. What are the features of green buildings that make them different from conventional buildings? These are features such as sustainable energy, waste management, building materials and so on. Before I come to that, let's start with a couple of definitions. What exactly do we mean by a green building?

7.5

A green building can be defined as: 'one which uses less water, optimizes energy efficiency, uses sustainable building materials, generates less waste and provides healthier spaces for occupants as compared to a conventional building.'

I'll go through each of those points briefly. Firstly, water use – a green building aims to reduce water demand. This can be done by using rainwater, for example, having a facility on the building to collect it. And secondly, by recycling waste water. Waste water from the building is collected, purified, and then recycled within the building. Now energy efficiency – perhaps the most important goal of a green architect. Energy efficiency means cutting down on the energy used by the occupants of the building. This can be done in a number of ways. One is to make use of alternative sources of energy – such as solar power, wind turbines. Another is to reduce the amount of energy used. For example, using natural light where possible, or materials which insulate the building, that is to say, stop heat leaving the building. Thirdly, let's look at sustainable building materials. Now this term 'sustainable' is an important one. Sustainable means being able to continue using something without it having a negative effect on the environment.

So sustainable building materials can either be natural materials like stone, wood, and paper-based products – or they can be recycled materials – building materials which were used before in construction. Finally, waste management. The aim of green design is to reduce the building's waste to a minimum. So for example, water from the building can be used to water the gardens. Other waste can be composted or recycled.

7.6

Now let's turn to our examples of a green building – the Pearl River Tower in the city of Guangzhou – that's G-U-A-N-G-Z-H-O-U – in China. It's an elegant building as you can see – a 71-storey skyscraper – over 300 metres high – 309 metres to be exact. It is one of the most environmentally-friendly buildings in the world. So what makes it so environmentally-friendly or green? Well, it's partially powered by wind turbines. It also has a number of features that reduce energy use, for example, solar panels and radiant cooling. Radiant cooling is an energy-efficient way of cooling a building by using water running in pipes built into metal ceiling panels.

Let's have a look at another green building – the Bank of America Tower. It is 55 storeys high and it has a height of 366 metres. That's if we include the spire, which is nearly 78 metres in height. The building is located in New York, in the heart of Manhattan. It was completed in 2010.

It is estimated that the tower will use 50% less electricity than a conventional building. Most of the lighting is natural light – the walls are all made of glass. There will also be a generator in the building which will account for 70% of the building's needs. The emissions from this generator – a gas-powered generator – will be cleaner than those from conventional sources. The building will use rainwater and grey water. Grey water, by the way, is the name given to recycled water from wash-basins. This can be used to flush toilets.

7.7

Well, in my view, skyscrapers are essential for modern cities for a number of reasons. The first is population density. A city with a lot of high-rise buildings has a higher density than cities with low-rise buildings. This means that less land is used and there is less traffic as people live closer to work, shops, etc. and don't need cars to get around. Let's look at Hong Kong and Mumbai as examples. Hong Kong, first of all, it has a population of 7 million but only 23% of its land is used for buildings. This means that the urban density in Hong Kong is very high, 70,000 people per square mile, but because of that the rest of the area is preserved as natural landscape for the people to enjoy. Mumbai on the other hand has a lower population density – 6,000 people per square mile, as it has a lot of low-rise buildings. As a result, Mumbai covers a huge area and getting around the city is extremely difficult. Another reason I support skyscrapers is …

7.8

A = Antonio   J = James   C = Carmen

A   Well, it seems to me that introducing the Internet in schools is not a good idea. For one thing, children will waste a lot of time playing computer games and chatting to friends online. What do you think, James?

J   I see your point, Antonio. There is a danger that students will do that, but I believe teachers will supervise students and make sure that they are focusing on the task.

A   I think teachers will find it very difficult to check on all their students. They have classes of more than 30 in some schools.

C   I agree with Antonio. It'll be very difficult for teachers to monitor students. Another thing is the expense. I read that it'll cost the government over a billion pounds to introduce the Internet in all schools.

J   That's not true, Carmen. The government will get local businesses to sponsor schools – so it will cost a billion – but very little of it will come from us.

C   But what will happen to traditional teaching? As I see it, students will spend all their time looking at a computer screen and have very little contact with teachers.

J   I don't think traditional teaching will suffer. There is a place for both.

7.9

Let me now turn to another example of green architecture and a very innovative example too. This is the World Trade Centre in Bahrain. A stunning building, I think you will agree. Completed in 2008, it is the first skyscraper in the world to have wind turbines integrated into its design.

The building in fact consists of two towers. Each is 240 metres high, which makes it the highest building in Bahrain. The towers are joined by three bridges – skybridges – and on each bridge there is attached a wind turbine – able to produce 225 kilowatts of electricity.

Each of these turbines is 29 metres in diameter – so they are very big and heavy too. Now the building is designed to face north so that the turbines also face the north. This is very important for two reasons: firstly because this is where the prevailing wind comes from, and secondly, unlike turbines fixed on the top of a tower, in wind farms for example, the position of these turbines cannot be changed. They are fixed in one position so they must face the wind.

Let's have a look at these turbines in more detail. How do they work exactly?

7.10

Another style of architecture which we should discuss is organic architecture. Now, organic architecture should not be confused with green architecture, though sometimes a building can be both. Organic architecture is architecture which takes its influence from nature and naturally-occurring figures. Unlike much of modern architecture, you see many fluid, evolving shapes and curved lines in the organic movement.

Casa Milà, a building in Barcelona, is an early example of organic architecture. Completed by the architect Antoni Gaudí in 1912, it is locally known as 'La Pedrera', or 'The Quarry' in English, because it looks like the face of a cliff where stone has been cut away. Many of the windows and doors look like caves. It is a unique space.

But there can be more to organic architecture. You see, as the buildings take their influence from nature, an organic building is usually designed to fit in well in its environment. In a city, this is not so important, but when a building is built in the countryside, or a place of natural beauty, an organic approach is often considered.

A building in America known as 'Fallingwater', designed by the architect Frank Lloyd Wright, is a good example, I think. The building is set, quite dramatically, in the middle of a forest at the top of a small waterfall. Now if you haven't seen this building, I can imagine that it sounds quite out of place. But the building makes good use of local materials. The façade – the exterior – is mostly covered in grey stone from the site and glass, which reflects views of the forest. The interior spaces are panelled with local wood. According to the architect the house allowed people to 'live with the waterfall' rather than just being able to look at it. This idea is important in organic architecture – being together 'with' nature, rather than just next to it.

8.1

Hello, welcome to another edition of Business Now.

Today we are looking at sports sponsorship – what is it? – and – is it a good thing for sport? The relationship between sponsorship and sport began in the USA in the 1930s when baseball became televised. Since then, it has grown dramatically and has spread all over the world and into most professional sports. In the 2010 World Cup, for example, sponsorship earned $1.6 billion for FIFA, the ruling body of world football. But who exactly benefits from this commercialization of sport? Is it good for the sponsors? What about TV companies – what profits do they get? Is it good for the sports – football, baseball, cricket, etc? Does it benefit all sportsmen and women, or only the Cristiano Ronaldos – a very successful few? And finally, what about the spectator? What do these loyal supporters get out of sponsorship?

(◉) 8.2 [including 8.3]

P = Presenter   L = Leo Desa

P I put some of these questions to Leo Desa, author of the book *The Business of Sport*. First of all I asked him for a definition. I'd like to start by asking you to define sports sponsorship. What is it exactly?

L It's actually a business relationship between – on the one hand – a provider of funds, usually a company – and on the other a sportsman or woman, such as Rafael Nadal, the tennis player. Or it could be a team or an organization such as Manchester United, which is well known around the world. So individuals and also teams can be sponsored. And we mustn't forget sporting events such as the World Cup and the Olympic Games. They can also be sponsored. Companies pay a lot of money to sponsor events like these. You may remember that FIFA, the world football ruling body, made $1.6 billion from sponsorship for the 2010 World Cup through companies such as Nike, Hyundai, Visa, Coca Cola, etc.

P Hmm. So sponsoring these major events seems to be a very expensive business. That leads me to my next question. What exactly do these companies get out of this sponsorship? It's not a form of charity, is it?

L No, it is certainly not charity. Sponsorship is really marketing – sports marketing. It combines advertising, sales promotion and public relations. Advertising is getting the brand name recognized – and of course some of these events have huge audiences – sometimes billions of people. Hopefully this translates itself into sales and profits. Public relations is important too. People all around the world like events such as the World Cup or the Olympics – in fact they like sport in general. So it is good for a company's image to be seen supporting these popular events.

P Which sports attract the most sponsorship?

L It depends on which part of the world you're talking about. In the USA, baseball and basketball attract the biggest sponsorship. In the Indian subcontinent, it is cricket. Motor racing, especially Formula One, is popular internationally in many countries. And of course there is football. Football is the most popular international sport and attracts a huge amount of money. Sponsors pay a lot to be associated with successful teams, such as Inter Milan, and also big competitions – like the World Cup, which I mentioned earlier. They also sponsor local football leagues – like the Premiership in the UK, which is sponsored by Barclays Bank. Also football stadiums such as the Emirates stadium in London are also sponsored.

[8.3 starts] **P** Now I'd like to turn to the question of the effect of sponsorship on sports. Has it all been beneficial? A good thing for sport?

L Well, on the positive side, it has brought money into several popular sports. This has meant that facilities can be improved – better stadiums, for example. And more people can see the sports through TV deals. It has raised standards in the sport. If a team has more money, it will attract better players and so the standard of the team should be higher. Also, if individual sportsmen and women are sponsored, they may be able to give up work so they can concentrate on their sport – running, golf, tennis, etc.

P OK, that's the positive side of sponsorship but what about the downside? A lot of people say that commercialization has ruined many sports.

L Yes, a lot of people say that. They don't like to see advertising around the edge of a playing field or the names of sponsors on the team shirt or on a cap. But it is an exaggeration to say that these sports have been ruined. Critics also point out that sponsors just concentrate on the big sports, football, motor racing, golf, tennis, baseball, and they neglect the smaller sports – such as hockey, and athletics. I think that is true to some extent. We can see that the gap between the two is getting wider.

P Aren't sponsors becoming too powerful?

L In some sports, yes, they want to change the times that sports are played, and in the case of cricket for example, they want to change the rules of the game, so that the game becomes more entertaining. By doing this they hope to attract more spectators to the stadiums and also to get a bigger TV audience.

P Isn't that a good thing?

L On the whole I think it is, but sponsors have to be careful that they don't change the game too much. And finally, some sports become too dependent on sponsorship, so if they lose their sponsors, then the sport can go into decline.

P So to conclude, Leo, what is the future of sports sponsorship? How do you see it developing in the next five, ten years?

L I think sports sponsorship will continue to grow. But the dangers are that it will focus on just a few sports or a few sports personalities. It has to be carefully controlled and we must make sure that the benefits are spread out to all sports. [8.3 ends]

(◉) 8.4

Have you ever wondered what makes a champion? In today's talk I want to look at the possible reasons that some sportsmen or women perform better than others. I'll be looking at the following factors: physiology – how the body works best, nutrition – what to eat and when if you want to do well in sports, sports technology – the equipment that is used in sports and training, performance analysis – that is studying what good sportsmen do and finally, psychology – what role psychological factors play. By the end of the lecture we will know what it takes to be the perfect champion.

(◉) 8.5

Let's begin with physiology. It can be described as the study of how an athlete's body works – especially as it approaches the limits – the limits of what a person is able to do when running, jumping, swimming and so on. So basically, the more we can learn about the body the more we can help athletes. We can help them to train – but also to improve their performances – to run faster, to jump higher, and so on.

Now a second important factor is nutrition. Nutrition means the food and drink we put into the athlete's body. What food and drink works best for the athlete – and when is the best time to eat and drink – and how much? Questions like these. Nutrients can be broken down into three classes: fats, carbohydrates and proteins. It is generally thought that carbohydrates – foods like rice, potatoes, pasta – are the main source of fuel for athletes.

The next factor is sports technology – the type of equipment, for example, shoes for a runner and racquets for tennis players. A lot of research goes into improving sports equipment. Let's take the tennis racquet as an example. Originally these were made of wood, but later, in order to make racquets stronger, other materials were used – first steel and later aluminium. Today they are made of a mixture of carbon fibre, fibreglass and metals such as titanium. So that's just one example of how science has been used to improve the equipment that is used by sportsmen and women.

Let's move on to another area of scientific research – performance analysis. This is an area of Sports Science that helps sportspeople and their coaches improve performance by providing a record of performance – usually using statistical information and video. This evidence is then used to evaluate and improve performance. Does it work? Yes, research shows that providing athletes with accurate feedback, based on systematic and objective analysis, is a key factor in improving sporting performance.

A final factor is that of psychology. Sports psychology is the study of the psychological factors that affect performance in sport, exercise, and physical activity. It deals with increasing performance by managing emotions and minimizing the psychological effects of injury and poor performance. Some of the most important skills taught are setting goals, relaxation techniques, visualization, concentration, and confidence.

8.6

To conclude, top athletes don't become champions by chance – or through luck. They work hard at it, day after day, though training and exercising. But in addition to this they get help from science. As I have mentioned, science helps them in a number of ways – it tells them how to move their bodies, it tells them how to train and exercise, and what equipment to use. It also tells them about nutrition – what they should eat and drink – and when. Finally it helps them to be mentally ready for sporting events. It is a combination of these factors that leads to sporting success and produces champions.

8.7

A Hello … er … Mr … er … Tendulka.
B Chakrabati, actually.
A Oh, yes, yes, Mr Tendulka is next after you. Can you tell me something about your company Mr Chakrabati? When was it founded?
B In 1957, in London.
A How many stores do you have now?
B Over 4000.
A What about sports sponsorship? Do you sponsor sport?
B Yes, we do.
A What sports?
B Football. We have a contract with a team in the English Premier League.
A But according to my notes you sponsor cricket.
B No that was a few years ago. That contract came to an end in 2008 and since then we have only sponsored football.

A Hello, Mr Chakrabati, very pleased to meet you. My name's Jason Brown.
B How do you do Mr Brown?
A Thank you so much for agreeing to be interviewed. As I said in my letter we are working on a project on the relationship between business and sport. First of all I'd like to get some background information on your company and then later I'd like to look at sports sponsorship in more detail.
B That's fine.
A I've been reading about your company, could you tell me a bit about the history – the early days?
B Well, it was founded in 1957, in London as a food importer. We started with just one major store but by 1980 we had fifty stores, mainly supermarkets in the south of England and, by the year 1990 we had more than 400 stores all over the country.
A And now I believe the number is more than 4000?
B Yes, that's right and that includes several overseas supermarkets in the Middle East, Europe and Asia.
A That's very impressive!

8.8

How many here people play tennis? Hmm – just one or two. How many people like to watch tennis on TV? Oh, quite a few! And how many people hate tennis? Only one! Good, because today I'm going to be talking about tennis – in particular about tennis racquets. I'll be looking at the way science has changed the shape of the racquets we use to play tennis. I'll start off by looking at the very first tennis racquets – big, heavy, wooden racquets that weighed a tonne. Then I'm going to look at the first metal racquets and what a technological breakthrough they were – steel and later aluminium racquets. After that, I will look in some detail at modern racquets – and how science has played a part in creating strong and very light racquets using a mixture of carbon, fibreglass and some metals. Lastly, I will be asking the question 'What about the future of tennis racquets?' How far can science go in producing the perfect racquet?

8.9

P = Presenter   D = Darren

P Hi again from the Sports Business Outlook podcast. Today we're discussing sponsorship with Darren Lewis, Director of Marketing at All-Pro, the sports clothing company. Hello and welcome, Darren. I'd like to start by asking you about the benefits of sponsorship for your company?
D Well, I think most marketing people in our industry would agree that sponsoring professional athletes and having them publically endorse products is quite essential really. We want to sell our line of sports clothing to people who do sport, and if those people see the professional athletes that they admire, wearing our brand of clothing, that is very good publicity for us.
P Could we turn to the question of how you decide which athletes you would like to sponsor?
D Obviously it's important that the athletes we sponsor are successful. We want to be associated with the winners. But there's actually more to it that just that. We often look for athletes who have a certain image. It helps if they're good-looking or have a lot of charisma, generally the kind of person that people want to be like.
P OK, well that's sponsoring individuals, but could we move on to the sponsorship of whole teams and clubs.
D Well, sponsoring teams has even more advantages – a larger audience who will see our logo, access to more athletes, side benefits like free tickets to matches, which we can pass on to clients. But of course, there's usually a lot more money involved than with individuals.
P Yes, well that sort of leads me to my final question. What do you think are some of the risks involved in sponsoring athletes?
D Well, there are definitely risks involved. If an athlete has a serious injury and has to stop playing after a company has invested a lot of money in them, it's bad for both the athlete and the company. Or sometimes, even worse, if the athlete is involved in some kind of a scandal – marital problems, or legal issues – if an athlete is involved in these kinds of things, that can reflect badly on the sponsor and damage the reputation of the brand.

9.1

C = Chris   CR = Charles Robertson   YM = Yuki Masaoka

C In today's discussion we're looking at trends in population growth rates – the overall picture today as well as likely trends in the future. We'll also be discussing the possible factors involved in the rise or fall of population in countries or regions. I'm joined by Dr Charles Robertson and Professor Yuki Masaoka, both researchers in the field of demographic change. Dr Robertson, could we start with you, please? What does recent population data tell us?
CR I think what we see from current statistics is that, generally speaking, the world population is continuing to grow but at a slower rate. We are currently at just under 7 billion and most estimates suggest that this figure will increase to somewhere between 8 and 10.5 billion by the year 2050. At the moment, population is increasing at around 1.1% per annum, but this rate of growth is below the peak of the 1960s when it was over 2% per annum.
C This rate of growth is not spread evenly over the world, is it? Professor Masaoka?
YM No. What we see if we look at a map of the world is that there is a wide variation in growth rates. Some regions tend to have a very high growth rate, for example sub-Saharan Africa, while other regions such as Europe have a growth rate that is much lower – for example, near zero in Germany and Italy.
C Why is there this variation – by region or by country?
YM The picture is quite complicated and there are a number of factors involved. For example, if everyone stayed in their own country then the population growth rate would just be a reflection of births and deaths in the country. This is called the

natural growth rate. However, people don't stay at home. For one reason or another, a significant number of people move to other countries – for work, for study, or maybe as refugees escaping from war or economic hardship. So migration has to be taken into account to give the complete picture – this is called the overall growth rate.

C So these factors – births, deaths, and migration – are reflected in the growth rates for these countries?

YM That's right. Of course there are other factors involved, such as the standard of health care in a country, the effects of diseases such as malaria, wars, natural disasters and so on. These are the reasons why some countries have low birth rates and others have high birth rates – and also why death rates vary from country to country.

CR If we look at Asia, for example, we see quite an interesting picture. In the Middle East, in countries such as Oman and Yemen, the population growth rates tend to be high. That is mainly due to a high birth rate. In the countries of Eastern Asia the growth rates tend to be lower. I could mention South Korea and Japan specifically. There are probably many reasons for this, but it seems that people generally want to have smaller families. We can see across Russia and into several Eastern European countries that the population is actually declining.

C Is that a bad thing?

CR Yes, because a declining population generally means an ageing population – more old people and fewer young people – and that of course has economic consequences.

C But there are exceptions to this picture in Europe.

YM Yes, look at France and the UK for example. Here the population growth rates are a bit higher – higher than in Germany anyway. This is probably due to a number of factors. One is net immigration – the number of people entering the country is greater than the number of people leaving. Another factor could be that, on the whole, immigrants to these countries are likely to have more children.

CR We mustn't forget when we look at population statistics that there are other factors that influence change – hidden factors or factors that we might not expect. For example, a recent study showed that in India the birth rate falls when cable television is introduced to a village.

C So it is quite a complex picture. Now I'd like to move onto the question of why this study of population is important. Professor?

YM Governments need this data in order to plan for the future. They need to plan for their healthcare system, the education system, likely energy consumption and so on. So predictions about the growth of the population are very important. And if there is an ageing population as Dr Robertson mentioned, then this has implications too. There will be fewer people of working age and more retired people to support.

C Finally, let's come back to world population. What do you think is likely to happen in the future? Can the world's population really continue to rise at this rate, because surely it is quite unsustainable? Surely it can only lead to depletion of resources and perhaps wide-scale famine?

YM At the moment we see two trends – the world population is rising but the birth rate throughout the world is falling, as families, on average, seem to want fewer children. And sooner or later if this trend in birth rates continues the world population is likely to fall later in the 21st century, perhaps as early as 2040.

C That's an interesting conclusion – but it could be quite a long way in the future before we see a decline.

(◎) 9.2

1 Some regions tend to have a very high growth rate – for example Sub-Saharan Africa.

2 However, people don't stay at home – for one reason or another, a significant number of people move to other countries.

3 In the Middle East, in countries such as Oman and Yemen, the population growth rates tend to be high. That is mainly due to a high birth rate.

4 There are probably many reasons for this – but it seems that people generally want to have smaller families.

5 Another factor could be that, on the whole, immigrants to these countries are likely to have more children.

6 At the moment we see two trends – the world population is rising but the birth rate throughout the world is falling as families, on average, seem to want fewer children.

7 And sooner or later if this trend in birth rates continues the world population is likely to fall later in the 21st century, perhaps as early as 2040.

(◎) 9.3

Good morning. Today I want to continue with a talk in our series on world trends. Before I begin, let me ask you all a question – how are you, everybody? OK, most people said 'fine' or 'OK'. No what I really mean is how ARE you? How is your life? Are you in good health? Are you satisfied with your life? Are you achieving your goals? Can you pay your bills? Are you happy? All of these things go towards 'quality of life'. So, again … how ARE you, really? Oh, not so good! What I want to do is to look at quality of life around the world – is it getting better for most people? And, by the way, what do we mean by quality of life and how can we measure it?

So I'll start off by looking at a common measure of quality of life. It's called the Human Development Index – or HDI. I'll look at the global picture – where are the countries with a high HDI? And I'll be discussing the trends over recent years. And finally, I want to look at what opponents of the HDI say and then some of the alternative measures of quality of life. So let's get going.

(◎) 9.4

The Human Development Index, or HDI, is one of the most common measures of quality of life. This was launched in 1990 by the United Nations Development Programme. Before then the emphasis when discussing human development had been on income. But the aim of the HDI was to shift the emphasis towards other factors.

Broadly speaking, there are three dimensions to the HDI: health, knowledge, and standard of living. The first, health. This is measured by life expectancy – can people expect a have a long and healthy life? Secondly, access to knowledge. This is measured by the average years of schooling that children have or can expect to have, and thirdly, a decent standard of living. This is measured by the Gross National Income per capita, how much people earn in other words. The figures are collected for each country and converted by a mathematical formula to an index – a number from 0 to 1. So, 1 is high and 0 is low.

So which countries have a high HDI? Which countries come out on top? If we look at the information in this table we can see that Norway, Australia and New Zealand occupy the top three places. They have indexes of 0.938, 0.937 and 0.907 respectively – that's the data for 2010 by the way. Countries with an HDI of 0.8 of more are considered to be 'high development' countries. At the other extreme, countries with an HDI below 0.5 are considered to be 'low development'.

If you look at the graph, HDI trends between 1975 and 2005, you can see changes in HDI by regions of the world. We can notice two things straight away: firstly, each region has a different level of HDI – the line at the top in black, for example, shows the states of the OECD – the Organization for Economic Co-operation and Development – which includes most of the European Union, the United States and other countries, up from around 0.83 in 1975 to over 0.9 in 2004. And this green line in the middle here shows the Arab states – up from around 0.54 in 1980 to nearly 0.7 by

2004. Secondly, we can also see that overall there seems to be a steady increase in the index for all of the regions – OECD here, the Arab states here – East Asia here. There are however a couple of exceptions – Sub-Saharan Africa, this line here at the bottom. You will notice that towards the end of the period the increase in this region was only slight, whereas in the other regions, especially at the end of the period, the increase was substantial. Look at South Asia. It began with roughly the same HDI as Sub-Saharan Africa in 1975 but by 2004 it was well ahead – around 0.6. The other exception is Central and Eastern Europe – represented by this line here. For a few years after 1990 there was a sharp fall in the HDI, but since 1995 the index has been rising steadily.

What about predictions for the future? Good news! Figures suggest that this improvement in HDI will continue – in all regions of the world.

Now the index has been criticized on a number of grounds. Some people say that there is no ecological consideration – looking at the country's effect on the world ecosystem. Others question the scale – and that a scale of 0 to 1 gives very little room for improvement – especially for countries at the top end of the scale. And thirdly others say there is no spiritual or moral component – the index mainly concentrates on material well-being. A radical alternative has been suggested – instead of concentrating on Gross Domestic Product or Gross Domestic Income we should consider the Gross Domestic Happiness of a country. 'How happy are people in a country?' This is the question I tried to ask all of you at the beginning. Of course, how we can measure Gross Domestic Happiness is another matter.

9.5

1 I'd like to look at some numbers to put things into perspective. This chart shows the number of students from Spain and Turkey attending the Park Lane Language School in each of the last ten years. Overall, there has been a steady increase in the number of students during this period. There was, however, a slight fall in the number of students from Spain in 2006. This might have been due to early signs of the financial crisis. However if we look at the number of Turkish students, we can see that there was no drop at this time, which is surprising.

2 The results of our survey indicate that when school is in session, students tend to use their free time for either watching TV or for sport. Now, if you look at this table you can see that during the semester only a few students said they read newspapers or magazines in their free time compared to television and sport activities. It is likely that most students get their information from the Internet and so the habit of reading is declining. The results for free time in the holidays seem to indicate that students participate in a wider variety of activities during this time. On the whole, during holidays exercise is down, and visits to family or friends is up.

9.6

1 Since 1995 there has been a rapid increase in tourists visiting Belisla. However, there was a slight fall in 2008 due to bad weather in the holiday areas.

2 Graph 2 shows a strong correlation between the number of student visa applications and the school holidays. It's clear that students apply for visas when they are on school holidays because that's when they have the free time to do it.

3 The bar chart shows that five students usually work at home, two in the library, two in the computer lab and one outside. Therefore we can say that 50% of students prefer to study in their own homes, while only 10% study outside.

4 Sales of four-wheel drives increased sharply between 2010 and 2011 while sales of saloon cars fell slightly.

9.7

A We took a random sample of people shopping in the mall, male and female, young and old. Altogether we interviewed 50 people over a weekend. We decided to choose a weekend as we thought that there would be more young people in the mall at that time and we wanted to get a broad range of ages. We devised a questionnaire with a total of 15 questions. We wanted to include smokers in the survey group, so the first question we asked was to find out if they smoked.

B So to sum up, the aim of our survey was to find out what the attitude of people shopping in malls was to smoking in the malls. Our results tend to show that most people are greatly affected by smoke, and would support a ban. Even some smokers supported a ban. Around a third of our survey group didn't support a ban but thought that there should be areas set aside in the mall where people could smoke. What conclusions can we draw from the findings? In our view, the best solution was to set aside a special smoking area. Although just over 50% supported a ban, we feel this majority was not large enough to justify a complete ban.

C I'd like to start by asking a few questions. Firstly, how many people here like to visit shopping malls? Hmm. I see most of you. And how many of you find you are disturbed by people smoking inside the malls? About half. Well, in our survey we wanted to find out what people thought about smoking in malls – if it should be restricted – or if it should be banned. As you may know, there is now a substantial body of evidence which appears to show that passive smoking can be a cause of respiratory diseases and cancer and is especially dangerous for small children. As a result, smoking restrictions are being imposed in many situations, for example public transport and the workplace. We wanted to know if the majority of the public felt the restrictions should be extended to other public places.

D As you can see from the pie chart, half of our group were male and half were female. The ages of the group ranged from 16 to 80. And about a quarter of our survey group were smokers. When we asked the question 'How are you affected by smoke in shopping malls?' about 38% said they were greatly affected – and only 23% said they were not affected. It's interesting to point out that even some smokers didn't like the effects of people smoking in the shopping malls. When we asked about solutions to the problem, about 61% supported an outright ban on smoking in malls, as you can see from this table here.

9.8

So, we can see from this map that the area of highest population density is really focused in the north and centre of the continent – the Netherlands, Germany – the UK a bit to the west, though you can see from these light green areas that there is less density from Switzerland down through the Balkans. The countries to the east are also less crowded. The Scandinavian countries, to the far north, here, are in beige, as the climate there makes large regions of those countries less habitable.

9.9

OK, as you can see from the title of this slide, we're discussing the Human Poverty Index. Now the Human Poverty Index was developed by the United Nations as another way of showing 'standard of living'. It's quite similar to the Human Development Index we discussed, but is primarily used with developed countries, countries which are industrialized and have higher incomes, though of course this definition is open for debate.

The criteria that the Human Poverty Index uses are a long and healthy life, knowledge and a decent standard of living. At the top of the list are countries which have very low poverty, according to this set of criteria, for example, Sweden, Norway and The Netherlands. This next slide shows how the data breaks down for Sweden. So, as you can see, the percentage of people who won't live to be 60 years old is 6.7. The second figure down – 7.5 – is the percentage of people lacking functional literacy skills, and functional literacy skills just means the ability to read and write and communicate. And the final figure shows long-term unemployment, which in Sweden is a very low 1.1.

◎ 10.1

S = Sue

S Welcome to *Technology Input*. I'm Sue Parker and today's topic is e-publishing. Today we're in Hong Kong, looking at a new e-book service offered by a Hong Kong-based publishing company, Chance Publishing.
Chance Publishing has just launched a new publishing project – an e-book list. It means that readers can now download the latest books to their phones, computers, PDAs, and e-book readers. But in addition to books, the reader can also download other media content related to the book – for example, videos, pictures, music, and computer games. Some people say that this is the future of publishing. Now this is the question I want to explore. Does everyone really gain from e-publishing? Here is Jamie Lee, the Managing Director of the company, to explain.

◎ 10.2

J = Jamie   S = Sue

J I believe we are offering two things that are new. First we're introducing the latest books written by our own authors. So we are not just offering books that were written long ago – classics, for example – we're supplying readers with recent books. And secondly, we are offering multi-media with the book. This means that the reader can download books that are embedded with other media content – such as videos, pictures, music, games and so on. So it's a complete package. In my opinion, it makes the reading experience much more rewarding. Imagine reading a novel and also having pictures or a short video or an audio soundtrack to go alongside it. It's an altogether much more interesting experience.

S So the claim is that this e-publishing service gives the reader a more interesting experience. But what about e-readers in general? Do these devices – phones, e-readers, laptops, etc. – represent the future of reading?

J There'll still be people who like the traditional book for a number of reasons. Firstly, they say they love traditional books and why should they change their habits? But if a book lover has, say 200 books, then that represents a lot of space in someone's home or office. Now imagine if those 200 books could all be on an easy-to-carry e-reader. Travelling or moving home would also be a lot easier. A second point that is brought up is the question of reading text from a screen. A lot of people say they don't like to read in this way because there's too much glare. They find that looking at the bright light of the screen hurts the eyes, but modern screens have advanced a lot. Tests show that they're much easier on the eye – and the glare is reduced. Many e-readers nowadays incorporate e-ink, which is specially designed for electronic readers and has less glare than the traditional LCD screen. So I believe there will still be a market for traditional books and the two forms will exist side by side. But increasingly, I think e-books will take over a substantial sector of the publishing business. You only have to look at the sales figures.

S Well, publishers seem happy with e-books but what about authors? What do they think about this innovation? And what do they think about the videos and soundtracks that go with the book?

J It's true that a few authors are worried about this innovation, but, in fact from my own research, I find that most authors actually welcome this change. They don't see it as a threat. They see it as a challenge – a new way of being creative by using sound, and still or moving pictures with their books. They say, 'This is wonderful – it means we can do anything we want!'

S Let's look at the music industry for a moment. They were in a similar position a few years ago when the downloading of music from the Internet really began. Can we learn anything from the way the music industry responded to the situation?

J The music industry is an example of what the publishing industry should not do. As you know, the music industry was very much against the downloading of music – at least in the beginning. And some people say, 'Why should the book publishing business be different? Shouldn't they try to stop it too?' Well, as I see it the music industry made a big mistake. Instead of embracing – welcoming – a new market, they tried to stop it. And of course they failed. Downloading music was too popular amongst the public, especially young people. I really believe we should learn from the mistakes that the music industry made. The publishing industry has been in slow decline for some time now, at least in some areas of publishing. Therefore we should welcome the e-book and the new technology. It's a new market and it will bring a whole new group of people back to reading and that's good for everyone!

◎ 10.3

Each year *Technology Review* selects what it believes are the most important emerging technologies. The winners are chosen by the editors to cover key fields. The question we ask is simple: is the technology likely to change the world? Some of these changes are on the largest possible scale: better biofuels, more efficient solar cells and green concrete all aim to tackle global warming in the years ahead. Other changes are more local and involve how we use technology: for example, 3D screens on mobile devices, new applications for cloud computing and social television. New ways to implant medical electronics will affect us all and promise to make our lives healthier.

What I'd like to do in today's lecture, the last in this semester on technology, is to briefly review five of the selected technologies – new technologies that may become important in the near future. The five examples we have selected come from five different fields – from communication, construction, medicine, science and lastly the media.

◎ 10.4

1 The winners are chosen by the editors to cover key fields. The question we ask is simple: is the technology likely to change the world?

2 Some of these changes are on the largest possible scale: better biofuels, more efficient solar cells and green concrete all aim to tackle global warming in the years ahead.

3 Other changes are more local and involve how we use technology: for example 3D screens on mobile devices, new applications for cloud computing and social television.

4 What I'd like to do in today's lecture, the last in this semester on technology, is to briefly review five of the selected technologies – new technologies that may become important in the near future.

5 The five examples we have selected come from five different fields – from communication, construction, medicine, science and lastly the media.

◎ 10.5

Let's begin with communication and the way we go about looking for information. Today an increasing amount of information comes in streams – that is to say continuous data – coming from Twitter, Facebook, blogs and news outlets. Search engines such as Google are now trying to make use of this continuous source of information in the same way as they search the usual websites. This process is known as Real Time Search. Real Time Search is still developing but looks as though it has an important role to play in the future.

The next innovation I want to look at is solar fuel. Scientists are working on ways of using microbes instead of crops to produce fuel.

These microbes do not require a lot of water and they do not need good quality agricultural land. The result would be an advanced biofuel – or solar fuel – and this could mean a revolution in fuel production.

Now I'd like to look at another interesting innovation – green concrete. The production of cement for concrete, as you know, involves heating a mixture of limestone, clay, and sand using a fuel, such as coal or gas. This process generates a lot of carbon dioxide. Now what if we could change the process so that the cement absorbs more carbon dioxide than it releases? This is what scientists in London have done. By using magnesium in the production of cement, carbon dioxide is actually taken in by the cement.

The selection in the field of medicine is implantable electronics. Implants have been used for some time in surgery. These small electronic devices are placed inside a person's body where they can control a function of the body – for example, a pacemaker is placed in the heart to make it work better. The problem with these devices is that they have to be removed at some point – which means more surgery. One possible solution to this problem is the use of silk to make these implants. Silk is a soft material and is also biodegradable – it breaks down. That means the implant will dissolve over a period of time and disappear. Therefore, there is no need to remove the device from the body.

Finally, a technology which combines two media, social networking and television. Television has traditionally been a very passive activity. Basically, we sit on a sofa, we watch. As a result, television viewing has been declining in many parts of the world as more and more people spend their time on other activities such as the Internet and computer games. But social TV aims to make TV more interactive – so that the person sitting on the sofa is more involved. It combines social networking – tweets, Facebook, etc. – with TV. The viewers can easily find programmes to watch and share, and discuss the content with others.

10.6

1 Our course starts next week and ends in January.
2 The results showed that Osman was rather weak in Maths and Physics.
3 A note was made of the weight of the substance before and after heating.
4 The committee decided to wait for the report before making a decision.
5 The airport terminal was constructed using mainly glass and steel.
6 If a student plagiarizes a text then they really steal the author's ideas.
7 The principal aim of the presentation is to outline changes in book technology.
8 An important principle of chemistry is that it is better to prevent waste than to clean it up afterwards.
9 The site of the new airport will be decided by the government next year.
10 The sight of so many people in the crowded shopping mall made Sami feel claustrophobic.

10.7

A I think that e-books are just a passing fashion and in a few years they will be forgotten. I love paper books. I like to hold them and read them. Most people I know agree. A friend of mine bought one of these e-readers but after a couple of weeks she put it back in the box. She didn't like using it and now she reads ordinary books. I hate reading from screens – I haven't tried e-readers but I use computers all the time and I hate reading from the screen.
B I personally don't like using e-books. I have tried using an e-reader, and I agree that some of the features are useful, but I wouldn't want to buy one. I admit that the sales of some e-readers are impressive, but I wonder how long this will last. Interestingly, a recent survey of young people showed that young people prefer books when it comes to reading. It is true that online newspapers are very popular. But at the moment most of these newspapers are free. What will happen when readers have to pay?

10.8

A Today's talk is going to be about iPads. The iPad is a tablet computer designed and developed by Apple. It is particularly marketed as a platform for audio and visual media such as books, periodicals, movies, music, and games, as well as Web content. It weighs about 700 grams, so its size and weight are between those of most modern smartphones and laptop computers. Apple released the iPad in April 2010, and sold 3 million of the devices in 80 days.
B Today's talk is about green concrete. Concrete is a familiar substance. Its durable nature and versatile applications have made its usage ubiquitous throughout our cities. However, this primary building material is also extremely energy-intensive to make and transport, and produces a significant amount of the world's greenhouse gas emissions. Can the omnipresent grey substance ever be reconciled as a green building material?
C Hello. I'm going to talk today about smartphones and I have a slide of a smartphone – just a minute – sorry – not that one – yes, there. As you can see it's just like a mobile phone – but it has extra functions, for example – it has advanced computer ability. So it's a bit like a computer that you can hold in your hand. About 45 million people have a smartphone – 45 million. Oh, that's just in the USA – I expect it's more in the rest of the world – in fact, I can show you the sales of smartphones on this chart – sorry – this chart.

10.9

Another industry that is going through a period of change is the film industry. And the technology I'm talking about here is not used in the production of films. I'm not going to talk about CGI or 3D technologies, though those are undoubtedly changing film as well. No, rather I'm going to focus on methods of distribution, by which I mean, how film companies deliver films to home audiences.

There have been quite a few innovations over the years in the home video market. VHS went out in favour of higher quality DVDs in the late 1990s. Now at the moment, you can still find DVDs in rental shops, but a number of large rental chains have gone out of business recently. This is partially due to the popularity of services where customers order DVDs online and receive them in the mail. Then, after they've viewed the film, they mail the DVD back in the enclosed envelope. It's easy, and cheaper than renting a video from a shop, but even this distribution method seems to be nearing its end. The problem is that in the age of the Internet, mail services are too slow for consumers. Sites like iTunes and Youtube have made it seem normal for us to get content instantly. Thanks to new faster Internet technologies like fibre-optic cables, online video streaming is now available in many places. Online streaming lets you watch your desired film online, instantly. There are several subscription services available, where you pay a certain price each month, and then you can watch unlimited films. I think this pricing system, in addition to the convenience, will appeal to many consumers. I think it's quite probable that we'll see less and less physical media – like DVDs – in the coming years.

PHONETIC SYMBOLS

Consonants			
1	/p/	as in	**pen** /pen/
2	/b/	as in	**big** /bɪg/
3	/t/	as in	**tea** /tiː/
4	/d/	as in	**do** /duː/
5	/k/	as in	**cat** /kæt/
6	/g/	as in	**go** /gəʊ/
7	/f/	as in	**four** /fɔː/
8	/v/	as in	**very** /'veri/
9	/s/	as in	**son** /sʌn/
10	/z/	as in	**zoo** /zuː/
11	/l/	as in	**live** /lɪv/
12	/m/	as in	**my** /maɪ/
13	/n/	as in	**near** /nɪə/
14	/h/	as in	**happy** /'hæpi/
15	/r/	as in	**red** /red/
16	/j/	as in	**yes** /jes/
17	/w/	as in	**want** /wɒnt/
18	/θ/	as in	**thanks** /θæŋks/
19	/ð/	as in	**the** /ðə/
20	/ʃ/	as in	**she** /ʃiː/
21	/ʒ/	as in	**television** /'telɪvɪʒn/
22	/ʧ/	as in	**child** /ʧaɪld/
23	/ʤ/	as in	**German** /'ʤɜːmən/
24	/ŋ/	as in	**English** /'ɪŋglɪʃ/

Vowels			
25	/iː/	as in	**see** /siː/
26	/ɪ/	as in	**his** /hɪz/
27	/i/	as in	**twenty** /'twenti/
28	/e/	as in	**ten** /ten/
29	/æ/	as in	**stamp** /stæmp/
30	/ɑː/	as in	**father** /'fɑːðə/
31	/ɒ/	as in	**hot** /hɒt/
32	/ɔː/	as in	**morning** /'mɔːnɪŋ/
33	/ʊ/	as in	**football** /'fʊtbɔːl/
34	/uː/	as in	**you** /juː/
35	/ʌ/	as in	**sun** /sʌn/
36	/ɜː/	as in	**learn** /lɜːn/
37	/ə/	as in	**letter** /'letə/

Diphthongs (two vowels together)			
38	/eɪ/	as in	**name** /neɪm/
39	/əʊ/	as in	**no** /nəʊ/
40	/aɪ/	as in	**my** /maɪ/
41	/aʊ/	as in	**how** /haʊ/
42	/ɔɪ/	as in	**boy** /bɔɪ/
43	/ɪə/	as in	**hear** /hɪə/
44	/eə/	as in	**where** /weə/
45	/ʊə/	as in	**tour** /tʊə/